THE PRESIDENT
IS SHOT!

THE PRESIDENT IS SHOT!

The Assassination of Abraham Lincoln

by Harold Holzer

Boyds Mills Press

Picture Credits:

Harold Holzer: 19; 27; 30; 31 top; 75; 76; 117; 119; 124; 129; 140

Library of Congress, Prints and Photographs, Division: 11; 14 (LC-USZ62-14065); 16-7 (LC-USZ62-8840); 23 (LC-USZ62-331); 31 bottom (LC-USZ62-8840); 32 (LC-B8184-10454); 38-9 (LC-B8171-7765); 47 (LC-B8171-7765); 51; 52; 56-7 (LC-USZ62-8933); 65 (LC-USZ62-8933); 68 left (LC-B8171-7775); 69 left bottom (LC-B8171-7784); 69 right bottom (LC-B8171-7778); 70 (LC-USZ62-92592); 73 (LC-USA7-16837); 83 right (LC-USZ61-1938); 85 (LC- B8172-1431); 86 (LC-USZ62-52153); 100 (LC-USZ62-79084); 101 (LC-B8171-3406); 109 and back cover (LC-B8171-3403); 111 middle (LC-USZ62-12426); 133 (LC-USZ62-11193); 136; 142 (LC-B8171-1273); 144 (LC-USZ62-14841); 145; 158 (LC-B8171-7773); 160 (LC-B8171-7797); 169

Courtesy of The Lincoln Museum, Fort Wayne, IN: 3 (#2258); 15 (#4052); 25 left (#4017); 25 middle (#116); 25 right (#3816); 28 (#3313); 34 (#2792); 36 (#2210); 37 (#2209); 48 (#3993); 58 (#3526); 68 right top (#3465); 68 right bottom (#3463); 69 left top (#3466); 69 left middle (#1971); 69 right top (#3474); 69 right middle (#3461); 80-81 (#2800); 83 left (#0-27); 87 (#4039); 89 (#4036); 98 left (#2186); 98 right (#3138); 110 (#3140); 111 top (#30); 111 bottom (#2800); 120-21 (#1420); 125 top (#32); 125 bottom (#1420); 134-5 (#20); 138 (#3172); 141 (#3282); 143 (#1687); 146 top (#2380); 146 bottom (#43); 147 (#2017); 148 (#20); 149 (#2293); 151 (#4263); 152-3 (#MA 11); 156 top (#MA11); 156 bottom (#38); 173 (#2433)

From *Lincoln's Assassins*, Copyright © 2001, James L. Swanson and Daniel R. Weinberg, All rights reserved: 108

Picture History: 103; 113

Boyds Mills Press
815 Church Street
Honesdale, Pennsylvania 18431
Printed in China

Publisher Cataloging-in-Publication Data (U.S.)

Holzer, Harold.
    The President is shot! : the assassination of Abraham Lincoln / by Harold Holzer. —1st ed.
184 p. : ill., photos. ;   cm.
Summary: The brutal murder of Abraham Lincoln shocked America and changed
our history forever. Why Booth killed Lincoln and how the assassination
transformed Lincoln from man to myth is explored.
ISBN 1-56397-985-3
1. Lincoln, Abraham, 1809–1865 — Assassination — Juvenile literature. 2. Lincoln, Abraham,
1809–1865 — Juvenile literature. 2. Presidents — United States — Juvenile literature.
(1. Lincoln, Abraham, 1809–1865 — Assassination. 2. Lincoln, Abraham, 1809–1865.
3. Presidents.) I. Title
973.7/092 21   E457.5.H65 2004
2003112909

First edition, 2004
The text of this book is set in 13-point Minion.
Visit our Web site at www.boydsmillspress.com

10 9 8 7 6 5 4 3 2 1

About the Cover: The Assassination of President Lincoln, at Ford's Theatre, Washington, D.C., April 14th, 1865, *was a best-selling print by Currier & Ives of New York, which was issued a few weeks after the murder. It shows John Wilkes Booth (right) shooting the president from behind, with Major Henry Rathbone, Clara Harris, and Mary Todd Lincoln nearby. Courtesy of The Lincoln Museum, Fort Wayne, Indiana, (#3140).*

Dedicated to the memory of Michael Maione,
Ford's Theatre Historian

I cannot bring myself to believe that
any human being lives
who would do me any harm.

—Abraham Lincoln to General Edward H. Ripley
April 5, 1865, nine days before his assassination

Contents

Acknowledgments

The author is grateful to three respected experts on the assassination. These friends read this book when it was first written, corrected many errors, and offered important advice and assistance. They have made it a much better book for their efforts.

My thanks go to Richard Sloan of Seaford, New York, cofounder of the Lincoln Group of New York; Professor William Hanchett of San Diego, California, author of the fine book *The Lincoln Murder Conspiracies*; and especially Dr. Edward Steers Jr. of Berkeley Springs, West Virginia, whose 2001 book *Blood on the Moon* is now considered the finest book about the Lincoln assassination. I appreciate their help more than I can say.

Very special thanks go, too, to my superb editor, Carolyn P. Yoder, who now knows more details about the Lincoln assassination than I do.

—H. H.

Introduction

The Tolling of the Bells

Lincoln squints for an outdoor portrait made on the White House balcony on March 6, 1865, two days after his second inauguration.

First one church bell rang, then another, then another. Firehouse bells joined the chorus, and then came the sound of courthouse bells. Soon the glorious sound of bells—hundreds of them, singing out together like a gigantic orchestra—echoed through the city of Washington.

People began throwing open their windows, rushing from their homes, crowding into the muddy streets. Excitedly, they gathered in groups, asking neighbors what these loudly pealing bells could mean. It was Sunday afternoon, April 9, 1865.

It was also a holy day. The bells had rung early that same morning to signal the start of Palm Sunday worship. But church services had ended hours ago. The bells had not rung since, and they had not rung all together, nor so loudly or for so long.

Soon came the news, whispered at first, then shouted joyously. It was passed from person to person, carried along the neighborhoods by happy teenagers racing through the streets. It was repeated breathlessly by long-suffering wives and parents. Men and women were soon laughing and weeping together, shouting and embracing. After four long, bloody years of fighting, after hundreds of thousands of young men had died of wounds and disease, after so much suffering and sadness, the long-prayed-for news had come: the American Civil War was all but over.

The official report had just come racing over the telegraph wires from Appomattox Court House, Virginia, a tiny village some 150 miles to the southwest. Robert E. Lee had surrendered his Confederate army to the Union general in chief, Ulysses S. Grant. Washington's church bells had erupted to celebrate the Union victory and to welcome the return of peace.

Over the next week, the people of the nation's capital celebrated day and night. Fireworks burst over the city. Bands played music in the streets. Cannons boomed in tribute. Torchlight parades marched up and down the avenues. And the church bells rang and rang and rang.

Such happiness had not been seen in the city for years. And it was easy to understand why. No more battles. No more worrying about husbands, brothers, fathers, and sons fighting in distant places like Gettysburg, Atlanta, and Shiloh. No more suffering. No more bloodshed. No more death.

As it turned out, all too quickly the news proved too good to be true. One more man would be killed—and not just any man, but the man who had led the North to triumph.

This man had saved the Union, preserved American freedom, and defended the country that guaranteed liberty to all. He had issued the Emancipation Proclamation, which began the work of ending slavery at last. He had inspired the North with his eloquent speeches about the country's "new birth of freedom" and about "government of the people, by the people, for the people." And he had pleaded that Americans end their bitter war and reunite "with malice toward none; with charity for all."

But malice lingered in the hearts of some, and one more victim would pay the price. The last man to die would be the tall, bearded, sad-looking man in the black stovepipe hat and long black coat. For so long he seemed to carry all the suffering of the people in his face and in his heart.

One more man would die: the president of the United States, Abraham Lincoln. On Friday evening, April 14, 1865, less than a week after Lee surrendered, a popular young actor named John Wilkes Booth crept quietly into a Washington theater where Lincoln sat in the audience watching a play. There, as Lincoln laughed at a comedy onstage, Booth sneaked up on the president, took out a pistol, and shot him in the back of the head. The next morning, Lincoln died. He was only fifty-six years old.

Lincoln's coffin rested in this hearse during his funeral.

Now bells tolled in the city once again. They were muffled bells this time, ringing slowly, mournfully, and rhythmically, like the beating of a drum. They rang from church steeples bathed in springtime rain. It was almost as if the sky were weeping in sympathy. The music and fireworks stopped. Shops shut down in tribute. American flags were lowered to half-staff. Numb with shock and choked with sadness, the rich and poor alike hung black drapes over their doorways and lovingly placed Lincoln's picture in their windows.

Just one week earlier, a happy city had been in the midst of the grandest celebration in memory. Now, all too suddenly, it found itself awash in tragedy. Never before,

When news of President Lincoln's death reached his hometown of Springfield, Illinois, his old friends dressed his horse, "Old Bob," in black drape, and had him photographed.

one citizen observed, had so large a city gone so quickly, and so completely, from joy to grief.

No one who lived through that week would ever forget what happened—although for nearly 150 years, no one has been sure *why* it happened.

This is the story of the horrifying murder that ended the life of America's greatest president. This is the story of the tragic event that plunged the city of Washington and all the northern states into the deepest mourning in memory and changed America forever.

This is the story of the assassination of Abraham Lincoln.

Chapter One

Abraham Lincoln
and the
Civil War

Only five years earlier, back in 1860, few Americans even knew who Abraham Lincoln was. The Illinois lawyer had been elected to the state legislature as a young man and later served a single, two-year term in the U.S. House of Representatives. But he did not seek reelection to Congress and returned to private life. He did not seem destined for great political success, and certainly not for worldwide fame.

That would change. Lincoln was "aroused" back into politics, as he put it, by a law passed by Congress in 1854. The Kansas-Nebraska Act gave white settlers the right to vote yes or no on whether to allow slavery in new federal territories. Lincoln believed that slavery should not be allowed to expand anywhere in the rapidly growing country. He began speaking out in opposition to slavery and soon found himself back in the political spotlight. He believed that America was created "to give *all* a chance." He wanted "the weak to grow stronger, the ignorant, wiser; and all better, and happier together." This would not be possible if slavery grew.

"Equal justice to the south," he said, did not require northerners to agree "to the extending of slavery to new countries." Instead, Lincoln spoke of the "great principle of equality" and pleaded, "Let all lovers of liberty every-where—join in the great and good work" of stopping the spread of slavery.

The Lincoln-Douglas Debates

In 1858, Lincoln ran for the U.S. Senate and challenged his opponent, Senator Stephen A. Douglas, to a series of public debates. Although Lincoln lost the election, these seven debates increased his popularity. They were published in newspapers throughout the country and widely discussed in many major cities. Lincoln became known as an important leader of the new Republican Party.

In speeches in both the West and the East over the next two years, Lincoln spoke out forcefully against slavery. He argued that slavery should not be allowed to grow as the nation grew. No slaves, Lincoln declared again and again, should be taken to the country's new western territories. Slavery, he said, was evil. Although there seemed to be no lawful way to free the four million slaves

The Lincoln-Douglas debates attracted large, excited crowds during the summer and fall of 1858. Each candidate spoke for an hour and a half.

in the South, Lincoln hoped that by allowing slavery to exist *only* in the South, slavery itself would eventually die out.

These arguments convinced many Republicans that Lincoln could win the presidency of the United States. He was neither too liberal nor too conservative. He hated slavery, but he did not favor abolishing it immediately in places where it already existed. He believed that African

Americans should have freedom, but like nearly all white people of the time, he was not yet ready to grant them equality. He came from a western state and could attract many new voters to the Republican Party.

Still, he was not favored to succeed. It came as a major surprise when Lincoln won the Republican nomination for president in May 1860, defeating several men who were far better known. Many northerners applauded the choice. Lincoln, they thought, might well be able to stop the spread of slavery and speak out against human bondage until it could finally be destroyed. Most important of all, his admirers felt that he could win the election for the Republicans.

Log Cabin to White House

Abraham Lincoln was born poor, in a tiny log cabin in Kentucky on February 12, 1809. His father and mother could barely sign their names. His grandfather and namesake, the first Abraham Lincoln, was himself assassinated—by Indians. The Lincolns' cabin in Kentucky, and later their home in Indiana, had dirt floors and animal-skin windows. It was cold in winter and hot in summer. Lincoln's mother died when he was only nine years old.

Young Abe barely went to school for a full year—altogether—in his entire childhood. Encouraged by his new stepmother, however, he read books whenever he had spare time from his farm chores, learning spelling and grammar and discovering heroes such as George Washington. By the time he was a young adult, he knew many of Shakespeare's plays, and he read the Bible and poetry for pleasure. He could recite long passages from memory.

When he moved out on his own to the small Illinois mill town of New Salem, Illinois, Lincoln continued to struggle in life. He became a storekeeper, but his store went out of business—"winked out," as Lincoln liked to explain with a smile. He thought of becoming a blacksmith and for a while worked as a surveyor and as village postmaster. His only personal success came when he enlisted as a soldier in the Black Hawk Indian war. Although he saw no real action, his fellow volunteers elected him captain of their regiment. This "success," he later said, "gave me more pleasure than any I have had since."

Back in New Salem, Lincoln took a strong liking to a local girl named Ann Rutledge, but she died tragically. Ann's death deeply saddened the young man, but he recovered and soon settled on a career in law. In those days, few students went off to law schools. Lincoln had to study law books on his own, often sitting in the shade of a New Salem tree. He also ran for office for the first time. Although he lost the election, he did not give up. He eventually became a state legislator and a practicing lawyer. He moved to the state capital of Springfield, where he met, fell in love with, and married a spirited and well-educated young woman named Mary Todd. They had four sons, bought a house, and prospered. Lincoln built a solid reputation as a lawyer and made political friends wherever he traveled to argue cases. He became a leading attorney and politician.

The very idea that someone like Lincoln could rise from poverty all the way to the presidency of his country inspired thousands of Americans. What is often forgotten, however, is that although many northerners admired Lincoln and his views, most southerners hated him passionately. Lincoln's enemies called him a "Black Republican," meaning that they believed he sympathized far too much with African Americans. In the 1860 presidential election, ten southern states would not even allow Lincoln's name to appear on their ballots. In those southern states where his name did appear, Lincoln received only a few votes.

Lincoln won the presidential election anyway, supported by so many northern voters that he easily defeated three opponents. As he prepared to move into the White House, southern leaders plotted to answer his election by quitting the country altogether. Rather than accept Lincoln as their president, they would form a country of their own.

A Nation Dividing

Today it is difficult to imagine our country breaking apart over a fair election. But southern anger ran high in 1860 and quickly boiled over. White southerners were convinced that Lincoln would take away their slaves and destroy their region. They concluded that the only way to save their way of life was to leave the United States. They planned to secede from the Union and create a new, separate nation. Some southerners were not even willing to give the new president a chance to heal this growing anger. Before Lincoln took the oath of office as president, seven states voted to leave the Union. By the time he was living in the White House, four more southern states had decided to join them.

These slaveholding states declared that they now belonged to a new country, the Confederate States of

America. They elected their own president, Jefferson Davis, and set up their own capital in Montgomery, Alabama, which they soon moved to Richmond, Virginia. The southern leaders said that they wanted only to protect their own "freedom" to live as they chose. But in truth, what they really wanted to protect was the right to own other human beings and force them to work without pay. They opposed black freedom; they wanted slavery to live forever.

Lincoln rode to his innauguration with outgoing President James Buchanan(with hat). During the Lincoln-Douglas debates, Lincoln had referred to the president disrespectfully as "James." But when it came time to turn over power to Lincoln, Buchanan was helpful and considerate.

In the first days and weeks after he became president, Lincoln faced a crucial decision: should he let the southern states leave the Union and form a country of their own, or insist that they had no right to leave and instead fight to make them stay? Lincoln believed with all his heart that the United States must stay united forever. He believed that every American had a duty to respect the winners of fair elections, even if they disagreed with the results. He believed that if the Union broke apart, democracy would die in America and never flourish anywhere else in the world. To Abraham Lincoln, this was not a question of politics; it was a question of law, justice, and human rights. It was what America was all about. He decided to fight a war, if necessary, to keep the Union together. "We must settle this question now," he declared, "whether in a free government the minority have the right to break up the government whenever they choose."

On July 4, 1861, he told Congress, "I am most happy to believe that the plain people understand, and appreciate this." The fight to save the United States, he promised, would be "a People's contest." The goal of his government would be "to lift artificial weights from all shoulders . . . to afford all . . . a fair chance, in the race of life."

The southern states refused to back down. They organized their own army and declared that they would fight for their independence, no matter how many lives it cost. Few people believed at first that the result would be a long war in which hundreds of thousands would be killed. But that is exactly what happened. The American Civil War would rage for four long, terrible years. The vast numbers of dead and wounded soldiers horrified Americans both North and South.

Robert　　　　　Willie　　　　　Tad

The Lincoln Boys

Like most families of the day, the Lincolns collected
family photographs and kept them in a leather album.
But many other Americans collected photos of the
Lincolns, too, and kept them in albums in their own
homes. All of these Lincoln family photos were taken in
Washington after the Civil War began. President and
Mrs. Lincoln adored their sons, and some people
complained that they spoiled the boys. Their oldest son,
Robert (1843–1926), was away at college during much
of the war. The favorite child was Willie (1850–1862),
who died of typhoid fever in the White House. Mary
Lincoln never recovered from this loss. Their youngest
boy, Thomas (1853–1871), called "Tad" or "Taddie" by
his parents, ran wild after his brother's death. Another
son, Eddie (1846–1850), had died before his fourth
birthday back in Springfield, Illinois.

War and Emancipation

Southerners suffered greatly for their stubborn determination to leave the Union and protect slavery. Nearly all the battles of the Civil War were fought in southern states. Mile after mile of beautiful farmland and woodland was destroyed. Towns and cities were reduced to ruin, and many families found themselves mourning the deaths of loved ones.

To punish the Confederacy, the North also sent a fleet of ships to blockade southern ports and prevent supplies from arriving from Europe. Southerners soon had to do without medicine, cloth, paper, and other desperately needed goods. With so many southern men in uniform far away from their farms and plantations, their families found it difficult to raise and harvest crops. As a result, many went hungry. The residents of Vicksburg, Mississippi, had to flee into caves to escape Union bombing. They survived by eating rats. Other cities were forced to melt down their church bells to make cannons. One writer called this "the hard hand of war." For southerners, the war was hard indeed.

Still, the North could not make the South surrender. In fact, Confederate armies seemed to win more important battles than Union troops. So after nearly two years of battles and death, Lincoln decided that he must fight the South in yet another way. Using his powers as commander in chief, he issued his preliminary Emancipation Proclamation in September 1862. This, Lincoln's most famous act, gave the Confederate States one hundred days to give up their rebellion and rejoin the Union. If they did not, Lincoln's proclamation declared, their slaves would become "forever free."

Black Americans rejoiced, but white southerners reacted with horror and fury. Lincoln, they protested, was trying to steal their "property" and destroy their lives. No law gave him the power to free slaves, they said. They would defy him; they would keep fighting.

Lincoln signed the final Emancipation Proclamation on January 1, 1863. Just as he had promised, he ordered all slaves in rebel states free. He knew that by

FREEDOM TO THE SLAVES
Proclaimed January 1st 1863, by ABRAHAM LINCOLN, President of the United States.
"Proclaim liberty throughout All the land unto All the inhabitants thereof." —— LEV XXV, 10

Lincoln's historic Emancipation Proclamation began the work of ending African American slavery, but it infuriated many white southerners.

The Emancipation Proclamation inspired dozens of symbolic pictures. Some showed Lincoln personally freeing black people. Others, like this one, celebrated the words of the document itself.

signing the proclamation, he was changing America forever. "If my name ever goes into history it will be for this act," he told people as he took pen in hand, "and my whole soul is in it." African Americans called it the Day of Jubilee. From that day until the end of the war, Lincoln's armies set slaves free wherever they marched throughout the Confederacy. Lincoln believed that emancipation was the greatest accomplishment of his life.

But southerners felt otherwise, and their anger grew even deeper when the North began recruiting black men to fight in the Union army. Now black men with rifles would be marching into the South to kill Confederates. This infuriated southerners, and, as always, they blamed Lincoln personally. They stubbornly continued fighting for two more years, sacrificing thousands more lives, suffering and starving, but willing to give up everything to defend their right to own slaves.

Gettysburg: The Battle and the Speech

In the summer of 1863, Robert E. Lee's Confederate army invaded the North. On July 1–3, they fought in the biggest and bloodiest battle of the Civil War, at Gettysburg, Pennsylvania.

On the third and final day of fighting, Lee launched a bold attack on Union lines, but the famous Pickett's Charge failed to break through Union defenses. The Union won the battle, and Lee retreated into Virginia. More than fifty thousand men were killed, wounded, or missing. Most important, Lee had lost his best chance to force the North to accept southern independence.

Four months later, on November 19, 1863, Lincoln visited the Gettysburg battlefield to dedicate a cemetery to the soldiers who had died there. The president was not invited to be the main speaker that day. He was asked only to give "a few appropriate remarks." But those "remarks" proved to be the most famous speech of his life. At the Gettysburg Soldiers' Cemetery, Lincoln asked Americans to complete the "unfinished work" of the Declaration of Independence. All men, he reminded his audience, were "created equal." Lincoln concluded, "That we here highly resolve that these dead shall not have died in vain—that this nation, under God, shall have a new birth of freedom—

They Hated Lincoln

Lincoln was attacked by cartoonists throughout his time in the White House. Such pictures may have increased hatred for the president. In one cartoon, a cruel Lincoln is accused of asking for funny songs while walking among the dead and wounded on the battlefield *(opposite, top)*. Another cartoon hinted that Lincoln planned to make African Americans the equals of whites, which most white Americans feared *(opposite, bottom)*. In a southern cartoon, Lincoln removes his "mask" and is shown to be the Devil himself—just for issuing the Emancipation Proclamation *(below)*.

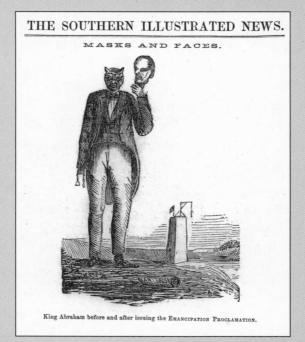

THE SOUTHERN ILLUSTRATED NEWS.

MASKS AND FACES.

King Abraham before and after issuing the EMANCIPATION PROCLAMATION.

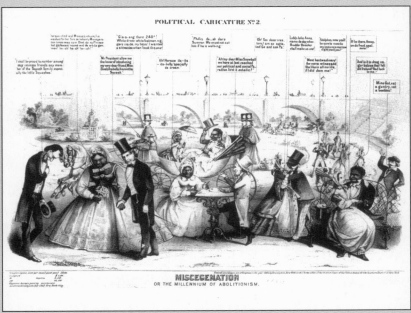

Lincoln arrives on the speaker's platform at Gettysburg on November 19, 1863. He is at the center of the scene, bareheaded and face down. He is about to give his greatest speech.

and that government of the people, by the people, for the people, shall not perish from the earth."

But the threat to "government of the people" was far from over. In 1864, with the war still raging, Lincoln decided to run for reelection. As he put it, using an old-fashioned country expression, it was not wise to "change horses in mid-stream."

After three years of war, not all northerners agreed. Many voters believed that the Civil War should have been over months, even years, earlier. Some thought that Lincoln had done far too little to manage the army; others thought that he had interfered too much. Either way, most voters were dissatisfied with him.

Running for Reelection

In the mid-1800s, candidates for president stayed home; their supporters did the campaigning for them. Nevertheless, Lincoln himself remained the main issue in 1864. His love of humor had become famous, but many northerners believed that their president should not be telling jokes or going to the theater to see plays while their husbands and sons were fighting and dying in battle. Others criticized his policy of arresting people suspected of treason and throwing them into prison without trials. Worst of all, the war continued to go badly for the Union.

For a time, both Lincoln and his supporters were certain that he would lose the election. Lincoln feared that if his Democratic opponent defeated him, the new president would cancel the Emancipation Proclamation, and that would end any chance that African American slaves could be free for all time. Most white southerners, of course, prayed for that to happen.

Fortunately for Lincoln, the North won some important battles just before Election Day. Lincoln's popularity suddenly jumped, and he went on to win his second term as president without much difficulty. He received 55 percent of the vote; nearly 80 percent of his soldiers voted for him. With the end of the war at last in sight, the Union celebrated Lincoln's victory. The Confederacy seethed with more anger than ever.

Lincoln noticed the rising anger, too. During the campaign, he told a visitor to the White House, "I began to receive letters threatening my life. The first one or two made me a little uncomfortable, but I came at length to look

ABRAHAM LINCOLN.   ANDREW JOHNSON.
PRESIDENT AND VICE-PRESIDENT.

Lincoln ran for reelection in 1864. The Republicans chose Andrew Johnson of Tennessee as their candidate for vice president. This is an election poster from that contest.

for . . . this kind of correspondence in every week's mail."

The president tried not to take the threats seriously. "They have ceased to give me any apprehension," he said, adding with a smile, "Oh, there is nothing like getting *used* to things!"

Besides, Lincoln could not imagine "what the Rebels would gain by killing . . . me. I am but a single individual, and it would not help their cause or make the least difference in the progress of the war. Everything would go right on just the same."

Ending Slavery Everywhere

One important thing did change: Lincoln and the Republican Party proposed ending slavery everywhere in the country, not just in the Confederacy. The Emancipation Proclamation had promised freedom only in those states at war against the Union. In loyal southern states such as Maryland and Delaware, slavery was still legal. In 1864, a Maryland slave named Annie Davis wrote President Lincoln: "It is my Desire to be free . . . my mistress wont let me you will please let me know if we are free. and what i can do." In response to such pleas, Lincoln asked for a new amendment to the Constitution making all people free and outlawing slavery forever. The Thirteenth Amendment was not ratified until after the president died, but it was Lincoln who began the effort to get it passed.

By then, even the most defiant southerners knew that they were doomed to lose both the war and their slaves. In their anger and pain, they continued to blame the man they believed had cost them everything near and dear. A small number of southerners were even convinced that they could win their independence if only they could destroy the one thing they believed stood in their way: Abraham Lincoln.

In contrast, to many northerners Lincoln now became a beloved figure. He was neither handsome nor well educated, but he inspired them with his heartfelt words. What was more, he had suffered greatly himself as a result of his determination to save the Union. Exhausted by his long, stressful days and sleepless nights, he now looked much older than his years. His hair and beard were flecked with gray, and he had lost a great deal of weight. He had black circles around his eyes, and he admitted that he laughed less often than before. He slept and ate little. He had a "tired spot," he wearily told his friends, that no rest seemed to cure. Most northerners at last came to appreciate, even adore, him.

In the South, hatred of Lincoln increased as the war

Lincoln's Family

Sadly, President Lincoln enjoyed little time with his family during their White House years. The crush of work simply took all of his time and energy. After the war, however, artists invented group pictures like these, making it seem like

This print shows the family before Willie (center) died.

dragged on. Desperate for one act of defiance that might save their cause, some Confederates plotted to get rid of the president. Lincoln knew that he was in danger, but he never backed down from his pledge to keep his country together. He told Secretary of State William Seward, "I would almost rather be assassinated than to have the Union fall."

father, mother, and sons enjoyed many such happy scenes. Mary Lincoln helped one artist create such a picture, thinking it would be better if history remembered them together. But in private, Mary admitted that she seldom saw her husband until very late each night, when he was exhausted from his day's work. And son Robert later said that he barely had a few minutes alone with his father after the Civil War started.

Here Mary is dressed for mourning, her family circle reduced by Willie's death.

Chapter Two

Why Murder Lincoln?

John Wilkes Booth was not the only person who wanted to kill Abraham Lincoln. Nor was he the first person to try.

Beginning soon after Lincoln's election, his personal mail often brought ugly threats. One writer called him horrible names and vowed, "If you don't Resign we are going to put a spider in your dumpling"—meaning they would poison Lincoln's food. An angry Virginian warned, "You will be murdered by some cowardly scoundrel." And yet another enemy wrote, "May the hand of the devil strike you down before long—You are destroying the country."

Mrs. Lincoln was greatly distressed by these letters. A friend of hers remembered that she grew so worried that she felt "danger in every rustling leaf, in every whisper of the wind." Her husband urged her to stop worrying. Little did he realize that as he began his journey from his home in Springfield, Illinois, to Washington, D.C., in February 1861, his enemies planned to kill him before he could even reach the nation's capital.

Visiting his elderly stepmother one last time before leaving Illinois, Lincoln found her as concerned about him as ever. She fretted about his safety. Sarah Bush Lincoln felt sure that someone would kill her son in Washington.

"No, no, Mama," he assured her, "they will not do that. Trust in the Lord and all will be well." And then he gently promised, "We will see each other again."

They never did.

The Road to Inauguration

Lincoln began his journey to the capital right on schedule—the day before his fifty-second birthday—and without too much concern. After all, he was traveling through the North, not the South.

In Westfield, New York, a small upstate village, he got to meet Grace Bedell, the eleven-year-old girl who had written a letter suggesting that he grow a beard. After his election, he had followed Grace's advice, and now he wore thick new whiskers. The newspapers reported that Lincoln "gave her several hearty kisses, . . . amid the yells of delight from the excited crowd" at the railroad station.

Reaching Philadelphia on Washington's Birthday,

February 22, Lincoln was invited to raise the flag over Independence Hall. He felt deeply honored. From his early childhood, he had worshiped the heroes of the Revolutionary War, especially George Washington. Now he stood inside the very building where the Declaration of Independence had been signed. Here he promised his audience that all Americans would "have an equal chance." As for himself, he quickly added, "I would rather be assassinated on this spot than to surrender it."

Real danger arose more quickly than he could have imagined. As the long railroad trip continued, detectives discovered a secret plot to shoot Lincoln when he arrived in Baltimore. The Maryland city was home to many slave owners who hated the new president. Lincoln's bodyguards asked him to take special care. Finally realizing that "people . . . were intending to do me mischief," Lincoln agreed to wear a long coat and an odd-looking hat when he changed trains in Baltimore. So disguised, Lincoln admitted, "I was not the same man." No one recognized him, and he escaped his enemies unharmed.

Writers and cartoonists soon poked fun at Lincoln for traveling through Baltimore in disguise. Some questioned his bravery and his ability to lead the country. Lincoln himself regretted the episode for the rest of his life. He later confessed to friends that it was one of the biggest mistakes he ever made. He worried that some Americans would think that their new president was a coward. But there can be no doubt that the plot to kill Lincoln in Baltimore was real or that his bodyguards were wise to insist that he take precautions.

Once in Washington, the danger facing Lincoln continued. He was told in advance that a sharpshooter from

Louisiana planned to kill him on the day he was inaugurated. That morning, March 4, 1861, well-armed soldiers lined nearly the entire route to and from the Capitol. Army marksmen perched on rooftops kept close watch on the crowd below, their rifles loaded and ready to respond to any threat. For Washington, too, was a southern city. Some of its citizens still owned slaves, and Confederate sympathizers and spies lived in many of its neighborhoods.

Lincoln showed no fear as he took the oath of office. "Why should there not be a patient confidence in the ultimate justice of the people?" he asked the large crowd in his eagerly awaited inaugural address. "Is there any better, or equal hope, in the world?" As if speaking directly to the people who wished the country—and its new president—harm, he ended his speech by saying, "We are not enemies, but friends. We must not be enemies."

Not all of his listeners agreed. Within weeks the Civil War began, and by summer battles were raging in nearby Virginia and in some of the western states as well. Lincoln remained in constant peril. "There was never a moment," wrote Lincoln's close friend and sometime bodyguard Ward Hill Lamon, ". . . that he was not in danger by violence."

The Threats Continue

Over the next few years, the president's mail continued to bring new threats of murder and new warnings of plots to kill him. Lincoln kept many of these letters in a large envelope in his modest White House desk. On the envelope, he wrote one word: "Assassination."

One such letter brought this threat: "Your days are numbered . . . You shall be a dead man in six months." The famous New York newspaper editor Horace Greeley wrote Lincoln in 1864 to warn him of "a conspiracy against you & this glorious Union." And another letter writer, who did not sign his name, scrawled this note: "Abe must die, and now." An admirer from New York State begged, "Beware of assassination!"

A long, rambling letter brought a warning so strange that it was almost comical. Its writer claimed that he had been hiding inside a barrel one day at a flour mill in West Virginia. While there, he had overheard some suspicious characters hatching a plan to journey to Washington to kill Lincoln. "The nation's life depends all together on your life," he wrote. "So I warn you as a friend to be Carful and watch."

But guarding his own safety was one thing that Lincoln tried for years to resist. Mrs. Lincoln's seamstress remembered that the president "never gave a second thought to the mysterious warnings" he received. As for the first lady, she was "sorely troubled" by the threats and took them seriously. The warnings frightened her and often gave her terrible headaches. She begged the president to watch out for his safety—for the sake of his family and his country alike. When an admirer sent him a thick oak walking stick, Mary asked him to carry it with him when he went out at night. "Mother [Lincoln's affectionate name for Mary] has got a notion in her head that I shall be assassinated," he explained to a newspaper reporter. "And to please her I take a cane when I go over to the War Department at night." Then he added with a grin, "When I don't forget it."

Ward Hill Lamon believed that Lincoln's "life was spared" only "through the ceaseless and watchful care of the guards thrown around him." To be absolutely certain that the president remained safe, Lamon volunteered to serve as such a guard himself. He took to sleeping on the floor outside Lincoln's bedroom, he later claimed, armed with pistols and knives, ready to fight off any intruder.

Lincoln's private secretary recalled that the president's friends and staff also advised him that he must be more careful. They would say something like this: "Now, Lincoln, you must look out and be constantly on your guard. Some crank is liable to come along and kill you." Lincoln would merely shrug and promise, "I will be careful." But then he would add, "I cannot discharge my duties if I withdraw myself entirely from danger of an assault." Hiding from the people was something Lincoln refused to consider.

Secretary of State Seward was convinced that "assassination is not an American practice or habit." He noted, "This conviction of mine has steadily gained strength since the civil war began. Every day's experience confirms it."

He could not have been more wrong.

"Public-Opinion Baths"

In a way, Lincoln was never fully protected, because he saw ordinary people face-to-face every day. Twice a week, he opened his doors to meet the public for three hours at a time. This was part of his regular routine. Crowds of visitors lined up outside his office for the chance to see him and to ask for favors or government jobs.

Lincoln liked to call these regular office hours his "public-opinion baths." He believed that they refreshed him. He felt that nothing else he did was more important, for the visits brought him into contact with "average" people. Besides, he pointed out, "they do not want much, and they get very little."

At first only a doorkeeper, a private secretary, and a few Union soldiers on the White House lawn separated these strangers from Lincoln. There were no metal detectors in Lincoln's time and little security. No one bothered to search the visitors for weapons or interview them in advance. In a way, Lincoln was lucky to have avoided an attack as long as he did.

Although he made only a few public speeches outside Washington while he served as president, Lincoln did go out from time to time. He was known to walk alone from the White House to buy a morning newspaper. He visited military hospitals to thank and comfort wounded Union soldiers. He occasionally spoke to strangers he saw on the street. He took carriage rides through the capital with the first lady. He often traveled the bumpy roads of the city to the Washington Navy Yard, where he watched inventors test new weapons and sometimes tried them out himself.

Occasionally, Lincoln traveled farther, sometimes to other cities such as Philadelphia, Baltimore, West Point, and Gettysburg. In Washington, he greeted soldiers as they marched off to war and raised the flag at ceremonies throughout the city. At least once, he journeyed—on foot—to have his picture taken at a nearby Washington photography studio. Today Secret Service agents carefully "sweep" all of the places that the president plans to visit. Well before he arrives, guard dogs sniff for explosives, and police officers search for weapons. Whole neighborhoods are often "frozen" so that the president can pass through safely. This clearly was not so in Lincoln's day.

Although Lincoln promised to be careful, he believed

that he could not do his job if he was constantly looking out for danger. "I see hundreds of strangers every day, and if anybody has the disposition to kill me he will find opportunity. To be absolutely safe I should lock myself up in a box."

The Lincolns at Leisure

President Lincoln loved the theater. Next to reading, it was his favorite pastime. Whenever he could, he sat in audiences along with ordinary theatergoers to see new plays and old, especially those by William Shakespeare. Once he found the time to attend three Shakespearean plays in one week. "Some think I do wrong to go to the . . . theater," he said. "But," he explained, "it relieves my heavy burden."

When the newly rebuilt Ford's Theatre opened its doors a few blocks from the White House in 1863, Lincoln began attending plays there as well. The building had begun its life as a Baptist church in 1833. When the church moved to a larger home in 1859, the old building proved hard to sell. Much as church elders hated all theaters—they believed that plays were the Devil's work—they leased their old headquarters to theater manager John T. Ford in 1861. Ford redesigned the building and opened it to the public in 1862. When a fire badly damaged the structure, he started all over again. This time, it took nine months to rebuild the playhouse. When the bigger, more modern theater reopened in August 1863, a month after the Battle of Gettysburg, a newspaper hailed Ford's as "an ornament" to Washington.

The new theater held seventeen hundred people in the orchestra section and two balconies. Elegant boxes above

Ford's Theatre in Washington, D.C., where Lincoln was shot.

the left and right of the stage offered special seating for important guests. The building featured a good supply of fresh air—especially important in warm weather—and a design so modern that even when the actors whispered their lines, their voices could be heard throughout the house.

Only a few days before delivering the Gettysburg Address, Lincoln went to see Ford's for himself. He watched a play called *The Marble Heart*, starring the well-known actor John Wilkes Booth. Altogether, Lincoln attended at least ten plays at Ford's while he was president.

During the Civil War, the Lincolns enjoyed summers in this lovely cottage on the grounds of the Soldiers' Home just outside Washington. This is the family's own picture of their beloved summer house.

The Lincolns in Summer

For at least five months every year beginning in 1862, the president and his family lived in a summer cottage about three miles northwest of Washington. The Lincolns' summer home stood within a compound known as the Soldiers' Home, a large community for disabled and retired army veterans.

The Lincolns loved it there. The weather was always much cooler on this hilly site than in swampy Washington. Their son Tad could run and play freely on the wooded grounds. Here the family was less likely to catch the diseases that plagued the city when it grew hot and humid. In addition, Mary Lincoln could relax, far from the public criticism that often followed her in Washington. She was unpopular among northerners, many of whom suspected the southern-born first lady of secret sympathies for the Confederacy—especially when one of her young half brothers became a Confederate general. Other critics spoke ill of Mary's expensive clothes and of the lavish parties she threw at the White House.

Whenever the family lived at the Soldiers' Home, President Lincoln had to ride to the White House every day to conduct official business. He was a commuter president! At first he rode on horseback, later in a horse-drawn carriage. Occasionally, he even rode through the farmland and city streets alone. Eventually, the secretary of war ordered a military guard to escort the president. So many guards soon began camping out at the Soldiers' Home that the president complained that he and his wife "couldn't hear themselves talk for the clatter of their sabres and spurs." Lincoln joked that some of the guards seemed so young and "awkward" that he was more afraid of being shot accidentally by one of them than of being shot by an assassin. He then ordered the unit reduced in size.

Defiantly, Lincoln sometimes slipped away from the White House or the Soldiers' Home without telling anyone. One night, he was riding back to the Soldiers' Home alone after a long and tiring day at the White House. No streetlights lit the area, and it was quite dark outside. Lincoln rode his horse at a slow trot. As he neared the entrance to the Soldiers' Home, he heard a rifle shot, and all at once his tall stovepipe hat flew off his head. Lincoln spurred his horse forward "at breakneck speed" and rushed inside the gates.

The president was unharmed, and he proceeded to joke about what had just happened. His biggest worry, he claimed, was being "separated from his eight-dollar plug-hat," and he wondered aloud which was worse: dying from falling off a runaway horse, "or as the tragic result of a rifle ball fired by a disloyal bushwhacker in the middle of the night." His friends did not find the episode quite so amusing.

The next morning, soldiers found Lincoln's hat with a bullet hole through it. Someone had just missed killing the president. No one ever learned who fired the bullet—a startled Union soldier, an enemy, or even a confused hunter—but the stubborn Lincoln still maintained, "I can't bring myself to believe that any one has shot or will deliberately shoot at me with the purpose of killing me."

Nevertheless, from that day on, Lincoln rode to and from the Soldiers' Home in a carriage, surrounded by soldiers. Security was increased, and he now had the additional protection of Washington policemen.

The experience did not change Lincoln's mind about guards, however. He still insisted, "It would never do for a President to have guards with drawn sabers at his door, as if he fancied he were . . . an emperor." Besides, as he observed one day, "if anyone wanted to kill me, he could shoot me from a window . . . any day when I am riding out to the Soldiers' Home."

"I do not believe it is my fate to die in this way," he said, and to allow himself to be frightened all the time would be like "dying all the while."

A Growing Danger

Not long after the Battle of Gettysburg began, Mary Lincoln was injured in a carriage accident. While she was out riding at a brisk pace, a wheel fell off her carriage. She was thrown from the vehicle and struck her head on a rock. When the president heard about the crash, he rushed

Mary Lincoln spent a fortune on clothes. Even though the nation was at war, she insisted that the First Lady must look glamorous at all times.

to his wife's bedside. For a time, her doctors worried that Mary would never wake up, but eventually she recovered. Some military men believed that an enemy had damaged the carriage wheel in an effort to injure both Mrs. Lincoln and the president, who often rode in the carriage, too.

Why was so much hatred directed at Abraham Lincoln? Why was he threatened so often? To understand the violent feelings that this now-loved president inspired, one needs to remember the fierce anger that had split the country apart and the horror of the war itself.

As the Civil War raged on, and as thousands of husbands, sons, and fathers died or were wounded in battle, some Americans blamed Lincoln for their personal tragedies. He was the one who had insisted that the Union must be saved. He was the one who had argued that the country must go to war. He was the one who had allowed the army to arrest civilians if they were suspected of treason. Southerners in particular held Lincoln responsible for their ruin, and many believed that if Lincoln were eliminated, the war would end, the Confederacy could become an independent country, and slavery could continue forever.

Jefferson Davis was president of the Confederate States of America. Some experts believe that he ordered—or at least approved—the plan to kill Abraham Lincoln, but there is no certain evidence of this.

Most of Lincoln's enemies believed that he would lose his campaign for reelection in 1864. Then, they hoped, he would return to Illinois, and peace would be restored without further bloodshed and destruction. In a way, when he won that election, Lincoln sealed his own fate. Now, his enemies reasoned, the only way to save themselves was to get rid of the president. If they could not remove him in an election, they would remove him with violence.

Besides, some Confederate leaders also believed that Union officials had on one occasion discussed a plan to kill *their* president, Jefferson Davis. Lincoln himself had supposedly approved the plan. Once Lincoln appeared to be threatening Davis's safety, some Confederates felt free to consider plans to harm Lincoln.

This was not the American way. These were not the classic rules of war. But America was now at war with *itself*. The old rules no longer seemed to apply. Brothers were fighting brothers on the battlefield. It was the most dangerous time in American history: for soldiers, for civilians, and even for the president of the divided United States.

In early 1865, Lincoln received a frightening seventeen-page letter in verse—a "last warning." The writer wanted Lincoln to know he was doomed:

> But Giant as thou art beware!
> To meet thy God, I say, prepare . . .
> Tremble Lincoln! Shake with Fear!
> It is God's True Sayings that you Hear.

Was the writer a harmless lunatic, or should he be taken seriously? Not long before, on December 1, 1864, an unnamed man from Selma, Alabama, had been bold enough to take out an outrageous ad in his local newspaper. For one million dollars, the man offered to murder Lincoln, along with his vice president and secretary of state. "That will give us peace," the ad said, "and satisfy the world that cruel tyrants cannot live in a land of liberty." Some Confederates really believed this. And that is why Lincoln's life was in such grave danger after 1864.

The Dreamer Has a Nightmare

President Lincoln believed in visions and dreams. One day, well before his first inauguration, he glanced in a mirror and saw not one but two reflections of his own face—one clear, the other faded. He told Mary that he thought this meant that he would later be reelected president but that he would not live to serve out his second term.

In the White House, just before great battles, he would often dream of sailing on a large ship toward a distant shore. Just days before he was killed, he had this dream again. But he could not understand why. The war, after all, was just about over. General Lee had surrendered. No great battles were left to be fought. Lincoln thought that his dream meant that some other important event would soon occur. "We shall, judging from the past, have great news very soon," he told his secretary of the navy. No one imagined that the "great news" would be the death of the president himself.

Shortly thereafter, Lincoln had quite a different dream. It was so disturbing that he told others about it the next morning.

He dreamed that he had been awakened by the sound of sobs coming from the main floor of the White House. Getting out of bed, he crept quietly downstairs, where he was astonished to discover that a large funeral was taking place in the grand East Room. Mourners gathered around the coffin, crying. Soldiers stood guard over the body. "Who is dead in the White House?" Lincoln demanded. "The President," came the reply, followed by a heavy sob. "He was killed by an assassin!" Those frightening words startled Lincoln awake from his dream, and he was unable to sleep for the rest of the night. "I have been strangely annoyed by it ever since," Lincoln complained to his frightened wife.

"This is horrid," Mary said. "I wish you had not told it. I am glad I don't believe in dreams, or I should be in terror from this time forth." Only weeks later, his family would remember the story with a shudder.

By that time, however, Lincoln was prepared to leave his life to fate. "I long ago made up my mind that if anyone wants to kill me, he will do it," he said. "There are a thousand ways of getting at a man if it is desirable that he should be killed."

One man desired it very much. His name was John Wilkes Booth.

Chapter Three

Enter John Wilkes Booth

Who was John Wilkes Booth? Why did he do what so many enemies of Lincoln merely threatened to do? Was he insane, or did he really believe that murdering President Lincoln was the right thing to do? Did he act alone, or did the Confederate government engage him to eliminate Lincoln? And how on earth did he succeed in committing such a crime in front of so many people?

What is often forgotten is that by the time Booth shot Lincoln to death on April 14, 1865, he was already well known in America. A handsome, talented actor, he had appeared onstage in major cities across the country. Pictures of him were on

John Wilkes Booth was one of the most photographed celebrities of his time. Like today's superstars, his picture was much in demand by his fans.

sale at newsstands and photo galleries, where fans eagerly purchased them. People often recognized him on the street. What was more, Booth came from a famous family. His father and brother also were celebrated actors.

Born to Star

John Wilkes Booth was born on May 10, 1838, on a farm near Baltimore, Maryland. His parents were not married at the time. In fact, his father, British-born actor Junius Brutus Booth, already had a wife and son in England. But seventeen years earlier, he had left them and sailed for America, where he started a brand-new life with a woman named Mary Ann Holmes.

John was the ninth of their ten children together. He was named for John Wilkes, an enemy of British kings in the eighteenth century. Ironically, John would grow up to be an enemy of an American president. And no doubt he would remember that his father had been named after Brutus—the assassin of yet another leader, Julius Caesar of ancient Rome.

In his new country, Junius Brutus Booth became the most acclaimed tragic actor on the American stage. Unfortunately, he drank far too much and occasionally suffered from periods of insanity. On his rare days at home, he was a doting father, and his children idolized him. The elder Booth hoped that his sons would not follow him into the theater, but both John and his brother Edwin did so anyway.

Junius Booth died in 1852 when John was only fourteen. Johnnie, as his friends and family called him, was rather spoiled. His mother and sister Asia doted on him. He went to private schools for a while, but he was not an especially bright student, although he did study hard. To friends Johnnie boasted that one day his name would be known throughout the world. "I must have fame! fame!"

he told Asia. He hoped that he would do a great deed that would make his name live forever.

So it did not surprise his family that after trying his hand at farming, John turned to acting. On the stage he hoped the spotlight would constantly shine on him, and audiences would applaud his every move. When he was only seventeen, he played the earl of Richmond in Shakespeare's *Richard III*. Perhaps it was no accident that his first role was that of a dashing young man who helps eliminate a hated leader.

The Most Handsome Actor in America

Booth began acting full-time in 1857, in Philadelphia. At first, worried that he would be compared unfavorably to his well-known father, he called himself J. Wilkes. At the start, he earned eight dollars per week, and he was terrible. Audiences booed and jeered him, but he would not give up.

Turning twenty the next year, he signed on with a new acting troupe in Richmond, Virginia. There he gained experience and confidence and quickly came into his own as a young star. Although he was short, he was extremely handsome, and women adored him. He learned to recite his dramatic lines with great force and his romantic ones with soft tenderness. His piercing black eyes penetrated into the farthest reaches of the theater.

Booth began to specialize in what today would be called action roles. He was very athletic and could leap onto the stage from great heights. His dashing sword fights thrilled spectators. First and foremost, however, he became a favorite of the ladies. "Booth's striking beauty was something which thousands of silly women could not withstand," one woman who knew him personally explained. "His mail each day brought him letters from women weak and frivolous." But Booth seldom read his fan mail, and when too many letters accumulated backstage, he simply ordered the theater manager to burn them.

His years in Richmond, and other southern cities, made Booth feel more and more a southerner at heart. Booth loved the southern way of life—that is, the wealthy, white southern way of life—in which slaves served white people's every need. Gallant young southern heroes were admired by white men and women alike, and Booth yearned to be like them. His greatest ambition, as an actor and a man, was "to be loved of the Southern people above all things."

In Love with the South

In December 1859, Booth found himself for once in the audience instead of onstage—this time wearing a Confederate army uniform and watching a real-life drama unfold: the hanging of abolitionist John Brown in Charles Town, Virginia. Two months earlier, "Old Osawatomie" had tried to ignite a slave rebellion at nearby Harpers Ferry. He and his followers had captured the local arsenal and barricaded themselves inside. Brown hoped that his actions would inspire slaves in the surrounding communities to revolt and join a crusade for freedom. But no slaves responded, several people were killed, and the effort collapsed.

Brown was captured, put on trial for treason, and sentenced to death. Meanwhile, his adventure sent shock waves through the country. Some northern antislavery men hailed him as a hero. But most southerners believed that Brown's raid had proved that the North was determined to abolish slavery by force.

Booth had oddly mixed feelings about Brown. He believed strongly in slavery, considering it "a happiness" for slaves and "a social & political blessing for us." But Booth could scarcely disguise the fact that he was also wildly jealous of Brown's instant fame—through the kind of grand historic act that Booth craved for himself. "John Brown was a man inspired," Booth marveled. He was "the grandest character of the century." Yet Booth also believed that abolitionists like Brown were "the only traitors in the land." He wanted them all hanged.

By coincidence, Booth achieved his greatest fame to date at the same time as did his future victim, Abraham Lincoln. In the fall of 1860, as Lincoln was elected president, Booth made his first national tour through the South as a leading actor. Leaflets praised him as "J. Wilkes Booth— a Star of the First Magnitude!—The Youngest Tragedian in the World." Crowds rushed to theaters to see him, and his salary shot up to four hundred dollars per week. At the very moment Lincoln was winning the presidential election, Booth was winning the hearts of audiences in Alabama and Georgia. Those states would soon secede from the Union in protest of Lincoln's triumph. While touring there, Booth surely heard many people condemn Lincoln and the North, no doubt adding to his hatred of both.

That December, as state after state began following

South Carolina out of the Union, Booth returned to Philadelphia, where he imagined himself to be the only man in the country who could both prevent war and save slavery. He wrote a rambling twenty-page speech, which he dreamed of delivering in town. It was filled with ravings about slavery and secession. In one section, he wrote:

> The South is leaving us. She has been wronged. Ay wronged. She has been laughed at, preayed upon and wronged. . . . The Abolition party must throw away their principals. They must be hushed forever. Or else it must be done by the punishment of her aggressors. By justice that demands the blood of her oppressors. By the blood of *those*, who in wounding her have slain us all, with naught save blood and justice.

Booth never gave his speech in public. If he had, it might have ended his acting career in the North.

The Role of His Life

Instead, Booth continued touring, appearing throughout the North as well as the South. In February 1861, the day President-elect Lincoln's train to Washington chugged into Albany, New York, Booth was appearing onstage in the same city. He was heard complaining so bitterly about Lincoln that his hotel threatened to throw him out.

As the Civil War broke out and then engulfed the country, Booth appeared in New York City, Buffalo,

Boston, Providence, Chicago, Detroit, Indianapolis, Cleveland, Cincinnati, New Orleans, Nashville, Washington, and back home in Baltimore. He went out West as well, to Iowa and Kansas, where he got star billing and earned a large percentage of the profits from his performances.

His letters to friends, family, and business associates were filled with reports of his own triumphs. "My success in New York continued fair," he wrote in 1862. From Baltimore earlier that year, he boasted, "Opened here last night a big house in spite of rain [and] snow." And in 1863, he reported from Washington, "I have just finished a fine engagement here."

Despite his stardom, his letters reveal a man hungry for even more attention. Booth wanted more from life than piles of money and a girlfriend in every town. He was a major celebrity, but he yearned for his name to be written in history.

Sometime around 1864, Booth decided to turn more of his attention to helping—and eventually avenging—the South. He was having problems with his throat, which no doubt made acting difficult. At the very least, he felt that he needed a rest from performing and could put his time to a more "patriotic" use. Booth gave his last paid performance in Boston on May 28, 1864, and set off on a new course. "The South wants justice, has waited for it long," Booth explained. "She will wait no longer."

Lincoln's reelection that November enraged Booth, who was certain that Lincoln would now declare himself king of America. "You'll see—you'll see" he warned his sister.

By this time, Booth had probably been working for months, perhaps years, as a Confederate agent. Because he

Settered according to act of Congress A.D 1865 by J.L. Magee in the Clerks Office of the District Court of the Eastern District of Penn.ª

SATAN TEMPTING BOOTH TO THE MURDER OF THE PRESIDENT.

J.L. MAGEE, PUB. 305 WALNUT ST. PHILAD!

Some people believed that the Devil himself made Booth kill Lincoln. This 1865 print seems to suggest that Satan joined Booth at Ford's Theatre.

traveled widely, it would have been easy for him to smuggle messages and instructions to southern spies operating in northern cities. In addition, when he went South to perform onstage, he could have smuggled medicine or other small supplies into the Confederacy. A man of Booth's fame would not have been searched by security men as he passed from North to South. Although spies normally work best in total secrecy, Booth may have found a different way to work for the Confederacy. Because he attracted so much attention as an actor, he attracted almost no attention as a Confederate agent.

In July 1864, Booth may have met secretly with a number of known Confederate agents in Boston. That fall, he spent a week and a half in Montreal, in a hotel that had been taken over by Confederate spies. If he was not part of the Confederate spy network before these meetings, he likely became an official agent after them.

In August, Booth met with two of his oldest friends, former Confederate soldiers Samuel B. Arnold and Michael O'Laughlen, in Baltimore. There they began hatching a plot to kidnap President Lincoln.

The Kidnapping Plot

Why kidnap the president? Since 1862, Union and Confederate armies had been exchanging prisoners regularly, with captured Union soldiers being sent north and captured Confederates sent south. But after General Ulysses S. Grant took command of all Union forces, he ordered prisoner exchanges stopped in April 1864.

What were Grant's reasons? For one thing, black men were now serving in the Union army. Infuriated by this, the Confederacy threatened to kill, rather than imprison, every black soldier it captured. At the very least, they would send captured black men back into slavery, even if they were free northern men. Lincoln and Grant did not want this to happen.

Grant also knew that the South needed men much more desperately than the North did. The Union could get along without the return of captured soldiers, no matter how cruelly they were treated in the South, because it had many more citizens and a steady supply of new soldiers waiting in the wings. The Confederacy, however, was running out of able-bodied men. Many had been killed or wounded in battle, and before long twenty thousand Confederate soldiers were being held in Union prisons. It made sense for the North to stop exchanging captured men.

This made Booth furious. "We cannot spare one man," he told John H. Surratt, a new member of his band of conspirators. Yet "the United States Government is willing to let their own soldiers remain in our prisons because she has no need of them."

Booth's gang continued to expand. Soon joining Surratt, O'Laughlen, and Arnold were George Atzerodt, a German-born drunkard; David Herold, a slow-witted drugstore clerk; Lewis Powell, also known as Lewis Paine, a muscular, handsome Confederate army veteran; and Samuel A. Mudd, a Maryland doctor who owned a farm on the road to Virginia. The group often met in a Washington boarding house run by Surratt's mother, Mary.

Booth was a born leader. For one thing, he was as charismatic to men as he was to women. Even though his ideas sometimes seemed outrageous and his plans wild, he was wealthy, generous, and great fun to be around—as long as you agreed with him that the North and its leaders were evil and the South and slavery were good.

The Gang That Killed Lincoln

John Wilkes Booth gathered this band of men and one woman to plan the kidnapping of Lincoln. Some of them changed their plans when Booth decided on murder. Ned Spangler only helped out on the day of the assassination.

Ned Spangler

Lewis Powell   *Michael O'Laughlen*

Mary Surratt

John H. Surratt

Samuel A. Mudd

George Atzerodt

David Herold

Samuel Arnold

President Andrew Johnson called Mary Surratt's boarding house (left), where the conspirators met to plot against Lincoln, "the nest that hatched the rotten egg." Today the house is a Chinese restaurant.

But Booth also had serious emotional problems. Like his father, he drank too much and was often depressed. He tended to view life as a drama that would end neatly in the final act. Although many of the people who knew him thought that he was slightly crazy, historians no longer view him as a madman who acted on his own to strike down Lincoln. Still, it takes a kind of insanity to kill a president, and Booth was at best an unstable personality. As the famous actor Edwin Forrest would declare when he first heard about Lincoln's murder: "All the . . . Booths are crazy!"

Crazy or not, Booth soon hatched a daring plan to

kidnap Lincoln. He and his men would ride up and seize him when he was on one of his carriage rides outside Washington. Then they would spirit him away through southern Maryland—which was filled with Confederate agents and sympathizers—and take him all the way to Richmond. There the Confederate government would announce that they were holding Lincoln as a prisoner and would agree to free him only if the thousands of Confederate soldiers in Union prisons were immediately released. It was a bold plan, but Booth believed that he could make it work.

Booth hoped that his scheme might save the dying Confederacy. Just as important, it might save slavery, which Booth saw as "one of the greatest blessings . . . that God ever bestowed on a favored nation." Besides, he said, he would consider it an honor to make for the South "a prisoner of this man, to whom she owes so much of misery." Booth used the money he had earned as an actor to support his band of kidnappers, rent horses, and buy knives and guns to arm themselves. Booth bought a small pistol for himself and practiced his aim every day at a shooting range.

Avenging the South

As fall ended and winter began, Booth followed Lincoln's public movements carefully, waiting impatiently for a chance to pounce.

In January 1865, he decided to kidnap Lincoln the next time he went to Ford's Theatre. Booth felt at home there. He was friendly with the owner and many of the actors and stagehands. He always had his personal mail delivered to the theater, and when he was in Washington, he visited backstage almost daily, even when he was not performing there. He was so familiar with the place that he believed he would be able to enter the presidential box, tie up Lincoln with a rope, lower him to the stage, and drag him away without anyone trying to stop him.

Booth was clearly having problems separating fantasy from reality. Whether he could have carried out this bizarre plot, we will never know. Although a presidential visit was scheduled for January 18, at the last minute a fierce storm struck Washington, and Lincoln canceled his plans to go to the theater.

Just a few weeks later, on March 4, Booth eased his way into the crowd gathering at the Capitol for Lincoln's second inauguration. He watched silently as the president passed through the Rotunda. Lincoln's private secretary remembered that Booth tried to force his way to the front of the crowd. Later, with his friend John T. Ford, the owner of Ford's Theatre, Booth found his way to a little balcony outside the building and stood above and behind the president as Lincoln rose to deliver his inaugural address. Had he dared, Booth could have shot Lincoln on the spot. But he was still fixated on his kidnapping plan. He had not yet decided to kill the man he hated.

Inauguration day started out gloomy in Washington. But just as Lincoln rose to speak, the sun burst through the clouds. "It made my heart jump," the president later said. Others in the crowd saw it as a sign from heaven that peace was sure to come quickly. As the thousands of admirers on hand strained to hear him, Lincoln spoke in a loud, clear voice about the sins of slavery, the terrible cost of the long war, and his hopes for the future.

Lincoln delivers his second inaugural address outside the U.S. Capitol on March 4, 1865. He asked for "malice toward none." Booth was in the crowd. Less than six weeks later, Lincoln was dead.

With malice toward none; with charity for all; with firmness in the right, as God gives us to see the right, let us strive on to finish the work we are in; to bind up the nation's wounds; to care for him who shall have borne the battle, and for his widow, and his orphan—to do all which may achieve and cherish a just, and a lasting peace, among ourselves, and with all nations.

Loud waves of applause and cheering rose from the vast audience. Then the chief justice of the U.S. Supreme Court stepped forward and asked Lincoln to recite the oath of office. For the second time, Lincoln was sworn in as president of the United States. For the first time, his future killer looked on angrily, only a few yards away.

Booth later regretted his lost opportunity. He told a friend, "What an excellent chance I had to kill the President, if I had wished, on inauguration day!"

Others wished it, too. Booth was not the only southerner planning an attack on Lincoln. A Confederate explosives expert named Thomas F. Harney was at that very time plotting to blow up the White House with a torpedo. He was on his way to Washington from Richmond when he was captured by Union troops.

Around the same time, Booth learned to his joy that President Lincoln would soon be traveling by carriage over unguarded roads to attend a play at a soldiers' hospital near Washington. An excited Booth organized his gang, gathered weapons, and rode out to choose the spot where he hoped to surprise and kidnap Lincoln. But again, the president canceled at the last minute. At the very moment Booth hoped to capture him, Lincoln was hoisting an American flag on a pole that stood outside the National Hotel in downtown Washington—the hotel where Booth stayed when he was in the city. The president was not in his carriage after all. And within days, he was not even in the city.

Lincoln the "Conqueror"

On March 23, Lincoln set off by boat to visit General Grant's headquarters in City Point, Virginia. While there, he met with the general and other military leaders aboard his steamer. It was time to begin planning for the end of war and the beginning of peace.

This picture shows Lincoln riding into City Point, the Union army headquarters in Virginia in 1865. But it probably meant to portray the president touring Richmond, the Confederate capital that he visited that April. Richmond, not City Point, lay in ruins, but with its slaves now free.

Just two weeks later, the Confederate government fled from Richmond, and Grant's army took the city on April 3. The very next day, Lincoln set off by boat from City Point to visit the place where the Confederate government had met for the past four years.

Unannounced, Lincoln stepped off a rowboat on the Richmond shoreline. Accompanied by only a few guards and holding tightly to the hand of his young son, Tad,

Gripping his son Tad's hand, Lincoln enters the onetime Confederate capital of Richmond, Virginia, on April 4, 1865. Newly freed slaves greeted him as their savior.

Lincoln walked quietly into the city. The smell of smoke filled the air. Buildings were in ruins. The streets seemed abandoned.

Within minutes, an elderly, newly freed slave stepped forward and squinted at the tall man in the black stovepipe hat. Suddenly, he erupted with joy. "Bless the Lord!" he cried. "There is the great Messiah! Glory, Hallelujah!" As if by magic, hundreds of African Americans suddenly appeared from behind buildings and swarmed around Lincoln, weeping, shouting, and cheering. Some fell to their knees to give thanks, but Lincoln, now in tears himself, pleaded, "Don't kneel to me. You must kneel to God only."

As the African Americans continued to cheer him, the white people of Richmond stayed silently inside their homes. Some people peered from behind their curtains, staring with hatred at Lincoln. But there were no attempts on Lincoln's life that dangerous day. "I walked alone on the street," Lincoln later admitted to his minister, "and anyone could have shot me from a second-story window." He seemed proud that no one had.

Lincoln also visited the mansion that Jefferson Davis had used as his residence. Lincoln sat in Davis's chair and then took a carriage ride through the streets, with well-armed Union soldiers riding alongside. He left for Washington on April 8. The following day, while Lincoln was still aboard his ship, steaming toward Washington, Robert E. Lee surrendered to Ulysses S. Grant.

For many citizens of Washington, the news inspired instant celebration. The city rejoiced with parades, bonfires, and, of course, the tolling of bells. All was "jubilant," Navy Secretary Gideon Welles observed.

The next night, Mary Lincoln watched proudly as "immense" crowds gathered on the White House lawn to cheer her husband. Mischievous little Tad Lincoln unfurled a captured Confederate flag and let it float in the breeze as the crowd laughed and applauded. Lincoln waved happily from an upstairs window and then surprised people by asking a band to play a favorite southern song, "Dixie." The Union had just won the Civil War, he explained, and "Dixie" was now the "lawful prize" of the North. Describing it as "one of the best tunes I have ever heard," Lincoln said that he wanted to hear it again. As the crowd roared its approval, the band began to play.

Not far away, Booth, his world now coming apart,

sulked, drank, and bitterly complained. Weeks before, fearing that his kidnapping plans had been discovered, his gang had broken up. But he refused to believe that the cause he loved so much was truly defeated. No one knows exactly when Booth decided that he must kill Lincoln, but this may have been the day.

"The Last Speech He Will Ever Make"

On the evening of April 11, Lincoln appeared at a window of the White House to read what turned out to be his last speech. Speaking to a happy crowd gathered on the White House lawn, Lincoln said, "We meet this evening, not in sorrow, but in gladness of heart." He thanked God for the Union victory and heaped praise on General Grant, the army, and the navy.

Then he slowly and carefully outlined his plans for peace. It was clear that Lincoln wanted the southern states to return quickly to the Union. He hoped that white citizens of the former Confederacy would again feel like citizens of the United States. But he also hoped that the right to vote would be given to "very intelligent" African Americans and to "those who serve our cause as soldiers."

To modern ears, this may seem like a very weak promise to a people who had suffered so much. But no American president ever before had even whispered the idea of allowing black people to vote. One person in the audience that night who recognized at once the importance of Lincoln's words was none other than John Wilkes Booth.

"That means nigger citizenship," Booth hissed to his friend Lewis Powell. "Now, by God, I will put him through." And then he vowed, "That will be the last speech he will ever make." He tried to coax Powell into shooting Lincoln then and there, but Powell refused. Booth would have to do the deed himself.

"The hour has come when I must change my plan," Booth now wrote. He knew that many people would blame him, but he still believed that one day the world "will justify me."

On Thursday evening, April 13, Booth stayed out late, watching in gloom as the city celebrated the Union victory and the end of the war. "Everything was bright and splendid," he wrote to his mother when he returned to his hotel. "More so in my eyes if it had been a display in a nobler cause. But so goes the world. Might makes right."

The next day, Booth would display his own might. He would murder the president. As he later wrote, "Our cause being almost lost, something decisive & great must be done."

Chapter Four

April 14, 1865

Good Friday, April 14, 1865, dawned bright and sunny in Washington. It was the start of the holiest period of the Christian year, Easter weekend.

One month earlier, a New Hampshire bishop had sent President Lincoln an idea for how the nation should spend this important religious holiday. The bishop had suggested that Good Friday be "observed as a day of Fasting and Prayer throughout the United States." He had added, "I have reason to believe that day would be agreeable to Christian people."

But it was not agreeable to Lincoln. True, he was a deeply religious man and during the war had become even more so. Although he did not belong to any particular church, he believed in God. He read the Bible almost every day and prayed often in the White House. As he wrote during the Civil War, "The will of God prevails."

But Lincoln desperately needed relief from the sorrow and pain of the past four years. He would not go to church this Good Friday. He would not fast or pray. He would not even answer the bishop's letter. Instead, he would go to the theater.

John T. Ford's brother, Harry, was thrilled to hear this news. Good Friday was always a bad day for the theater business. Few people attended plays on the holiday. Then he received word from the White House that President Lincoln would be coming that night to see an old comedy called *Our American Cousin*. General Grant would be coming, too. He could advertise their arrival. It would be a fine night for business after all. His brother, John, was out of town, so Harry rushed to the newspaper office to place an ad announcing the news. Ford was sure that the theater would be packed.

The President Begins His Final Day

On the last full day of his life, Abraham Lincoln awoke as usual around 7:00 A.M. He pulled an old robe over his long white nightshirt, put on his large slippers, and walked quietly down the hall of the second floor of the White House to the nearby family sitting room.

Anyone who knew him from the old days in Illinois would have been shocked to see him that morning. In his four years as president, he had gone from a young to an old man. He was frighteningly pale and thin. One friend worried that he now looked like "a huge skeleton in clothes."

Once inside the family parlor, Lincoln sat down and

From a Young to an Old Man

W hen Abraham Lincoln posed for the photo at left, just after his nomination for president in 1860, he was already fifty-one years old. But he looked young, strong, and eager to face the future. Less than five years later, posing in Washington for his last indoor photographs *(right)*, he appeared old, thin, and exhausted. The Civil War had left its awful impression on his face.

began reading a chapter of the Bible. He liked to begin each day this way. When he finished, he rose and walked farther down the hall to his corner office. The morning sun bathed the room with light. From the window, he could see the Potomac River—the river that had divided the

Union from the Confederacy, with Washington on one side and Virginia on the other. Now, Lincoln reflected, the United States was all one country again.

Lincoln sat down at the long wooden table that stood in the center of the room. At this table, Lincoln met regularly with his cabinet. And here, just two years before, he had signed his name to the Emancipation Proclamation. He had made history at this table, in this room, and he knew it. That morning, his early mail was already waiting for him. Lincoln began glancing at the letters.

The president received as many as five hundred pieces of mail every day. It was too much for one man to read. Before Lincoln saw any of these letters, his private secretaries went through them carefully. They answered some themselves and sent most of the rest to other government offices. Only a few letters were forwarded to Lincoln. On these, the secretaries wrote brief descriptions of the contents—just a line or two—so that the president would not have to read every word inside.

Nothing seemed to require his immediate attention that morning. There were a few newspapers, a few notes, and a check for five hundred dollars. Lincoln glanced at the rest of the mail, then took out some fresh writing paper.

First he wrote a note to Secretary of State William H. Seward to ask that the cabinet gather for a meeting later that morning at 11:00 A.M. It was Lincoln's habit to give Seward, his highest-ranking cabinet secretary, the job of alerting the others. Seward himself would not be attending the meeting. Weeks earlier, he had been badly injured in a carriage accident and was now confined to his bed, his neck and arm broken. Lincoln knew that the job of gathering

Secretary of State William H. Seward was attacked the same night Lincoln was shot.

the cabinet would be handled by Seward's able son and assistant, Frederick.

Next the president scrawled a note to General Grant, who was now in the city after accepting Robert E. Lee's surrender. Lincoln wanted Grant at the cabinet meeting, too. He had already asked the general to come to the White House at 9:00 A.M., but now he decided to postpone the visit by two hours. A messenger would deliver the note to Grant's hotel.

The president wrote a few more letters. The longest was to James H. Van Alen, a former Union general from New York. Van Alen had written to Lincoln urging him to be more careful about his safety. The general seemed greatly worried about assassins and pleaded with Lincoln to guard his life. The president was grateful for his concern. "I intend to adopt the advice of my friends and use due precaution," Lincoln wrote to the general. But the president also hoped that the time would soon come when Americans would not have to worry about such things. He told Van Alen that he wanted to build "a Union of hearts and hands," not just states.

His early-morning business done, Lincoln returned to his bedroom to dress for breakfast. Then it was on to the family dining room around 8:00 A.M., where he was delighted to find not only his wife, Mary, and their young son, Tad, but also his oldest son, Robert.

PRESIDENT LINCOLN AND HIS CABINET.　　READING OF THE EMANCIPATION PROCLAMATION.

Lincoln met with his cabinet on his last day alive. Though shown seated next to the president in this print, Secretary of State Seward was absent, confined to his bed while recovering from a carriage accident.

A Noble Face

Lincoln's son Robert brought this picture of Confederate general Robert E. Lee home from the war. He showed it to his father, who thought that Lee had a "good," "noble" face.

Captain Robert Lincoln had just arrived from Virginia, where he had served briefly as one of General Grant's officers. Robert had even witnessed Lee's surrender at Appomattox. Both of his parents had feared sending him off to war and had delayed doing so for as long as they could. Then they had arranged for him to have a safe post as an officer on Grant's staff. Now they were greatly relieved that he had returned home unharmed.

Filled with excitement, Robert showed his father a souvenir he had picked up in the South: a small photograph of General Lee. It is possible that Lincoln had never before seen a picture of the brilliant Confederate commander. Four years earlier, Lincoln had asked that Lee command the Union forces. But once Virginia seceded and joined the Confederacy, Lee felt he had no choice but to join his home state in rebellion. In those early days, Lee had worn only a dark mustache. Now he had a flowing white beard. The President studied his photo carefully. "It is a good face," he finally remarked. "It is the face of a noble, noble, brave man. I am glad the war is over at last."

Turning to Robert, Lincoln told his son how happy he was that Robert was home. Soon, he said, "we shall live in peace."

The president ate his breakfast. He seldom took much food in the morning: one egg, perhaps some bacon, and coffee. As Lincoln ate, Robert told his parents as much as he could remember about his exciting time with the army. He had loved every minute of it. Lincoln listened to every detail, but when the stories were over, he reminded Robert that he must soon return to Harvard College. The president wanted his son to study law, not as he had—by reading law books on his own, with no teachers—but at a real law school. Then, the president told Robert, "We will be able to tell whether you will make a lawyer or not."

A messenger interrupted their conversation to tell the president that the Speaker of the House was waiting to see him. Lincoln's breakfast was done. Ready to start another workday, he stood up and left the room.

The Lincoln family's own photo album contained this picture of the president's killer, John Wilkes Booth. It was probably collected by one of Lincoln's sons after the assassination. It is well worn, suggesting that family members handled it often.

The Assassin Decides to Strike

John Wilkes Booth slept late in his room at the National Hotel. And no wonder. He had stayed out much too late the night before, walking the streets in a daze as thousands of Washington residents celebrated the end of the war.

At around 10:00 A.M., Booth had breakfast at his hotel. Then he stopped in the hotel barbershop for a shave. Looking in the mirror, he saw a handsome face framed by black curls and a thick black mustache.

Just like Lincoln, his first "official" thought that day was about his mail. At around noon, he walked the four blocks from his hotel to Ford's Theatre to collect the letters that were held for him there. Inside, he heard people buzzing with exciting news: Abraham Lincoln and Ulysses S. Grant would be sitting in the state box that night to see *Our American Cousin.*

Booth could not believe his luck. The moment had finally arrived, and in the perfect setting for the attack: the theater he knew so well.

He rushed out to a nearby stable, where he asked to have a horse saddled and waiting at 4:00 P.M. He wanted it to be ready for him to gallop into Maryland after he shot Lincoln.

A bit later, Booth went to Mary Surratt's boarding house on H Street. There he gave Surratt a package to take to her family farm in Surrattsville, Maryland, about thirteen miles to the south. Inside were his binoculars. Booth planned to stop at the farm after shooting Lincoln. He also asked that some "shooting irons" be made ready for him that night. He expected that he would need more guns for his escape.

Booth's ambition was growing. Why settle for killing Lincoln and Grant when his gang could help him kill other Union leaders as well? With several murders, they could throw the entire government into chaos. There was

Vice President Andrew Johnson, for example. He was living nearby in a hotel called the Kirkwood House. Booth walked there sometime in the afternoon and left a hand-written note for Johnson at the front desk: "Don't wish to disturb you; are you at home? J. Wilkes Booth."

Perhaps the vice president would come down from his room if he received an invitation from such a famous actor. Booth could kill him on the spot! But Johnson did not respond. Never mind, Booth thought. We will take care of him later. Did he intend to murder Johnson that afternoon? Or did he hope to confuse the police by leaving a false clue? No one knows.

It was now nearing 4:00 P.M., time to pick up his horse. On the way, he met an actor friend on the street. Together they watched as a sad-looking group of Confederate prisoners were led away by Union soldiers. Their old uniforms were in rags. Booth was horrified. "Great God!" he cried. "I have no longer a country!" Booth handed his friend an envelope and asked him to take it to a local newspaper office the next day. The friend must not fail; it was very important.

Inside the envelope was a long letter. Booth had written it earlier in the day, perhaps in his hotel, perhaps at nearby Grover's Theater. He hoped that the newspapers would print it after Lincoln was dead. Booth believed that it would explain why he had planned the attack. He was convinced that it would make him a hero, and he hoped that it would inspire other southerners to rise up, perhaps even start the war all over again.

After learning about the assassination, Booth's friend, frightened, destroyed the letter. Years later, he remembered that Booth had written, "Many, I know . . . will blame me

for [what] I am about to do [but] to wait longer is a crime."
History, he wrote, "will justify me," for "this country was
formed for the white, not for the black man." Lincoln had
turned it into something else. If the South could be saved,
"it must be done quickly. It may already be too late."

"Right or wrong," wrote Booth, "God judge me, not
man."

The Happiest Day of Lincoln's Life

Meanwhile, at the White House, Speaker of the
House Schuyler Colfax found the president in a wonderful
mood. His cares seemed to have vanished, and he was
filled with "smiles" about Lee's recent surrender. He told
Colfax that the day Lee gave up was "the happiest day" of
his life. Then the two discussed the future. Colfax was
heading for California, and Lincoln wanted to know more
about the rich gold mines there. Colfax promised to report
back when he returned. Lincoln joked that he wished he
were going with him.

A few more visitors arrived: a riverboat captain who
needed money because he had lost his cargo to the
Confederates, a former congressman from Michigan, and
a new senator from Maryland. "It has been an *awful* war,"
Lincoln told one of the men. "But it's over."

Along came John P. Hale, the man Lincoln had just
appointed U.S. ambassador to Spain. Hale was delighted
to be going overseas. His new job would get his daughter
far away from Washington and that awful man she had
been seeing romantically—the actor John Wilkes Booth.

Lincoln shook hands with Hale and wished him luck.

At one point, a black woman named Nancy Bushrod pushed her way past the White House doorman and into Lincoln's office. She was upset that her husband was not receiving enough pay for his work. No one seemed alarmed by her boldness. No one seemed concerned that she could burst into the White House and then into Lincoln's private rooms. After all, uninvited visitors saw Lincoln every day. Besides, as the president kept saying, the war was over. So, surely, was any danger. Lincoln listened to Mrs. Bushrod patiently.

The president then decided to walk across the White House lawn to the War Department, where he often went to get news of the war. At the time, the White House still had no telegraph system of its own, and Lincoln relied on the telegraph room at the War Department for information.

On his way out, he ran into the wife of the manager of Grover's Theater. He had just received an invitation from her husband to come to Grover's that night to see the play *Aladdin*. Lincoln apologized. He liked Grover's and had seen many plays there, but he had already given his word to Ford's. To make up for it, Lincoln took his visitor to see the White House greenhouse and the lemon tree that had recently borne fruit there. Perhaps he would send his son Tad to see *Aladdin* in his place.

Then he hurried off to the War Department to find out whether there was any news from General Sherman, who was still trying to get a small Confederate army in North Carolina to surrender. There were no important messages from Sherman.

Before leaving the War Department, Lincoln asked Secretary of War Edwin M. Stanton if he might "borrow" for the night the husky officer who ran the telegraph office, Major Thomas T. Eckert. Lincoln knew how strong Eckert was and thought that "he would be the kind of man to go with me this evening" to the theater. At least that is how Eckert later remembered it.

Perhaps Lincoln was worried about a letter he had received recently from his old friend and bodyguard Ward Hill Lamon. Lamon had learned that the president had recently attended the theater with two men but no guards. Neither of his guests, Lamon had teased, "could defend himself against an assault from any able-bodied *woman* in this city." Lamon was angry. "*You are in danger*," he warned, underlining his words. ". . . And you know, or ought to know, that your life . . . will be taken unless you and your friends are cautious."

Stanton frowned when Lincoln asked for Eckert. Like Lamon, the secretary of war did not approve of the president's going to the theater. Without enthusiasm, he told the president that he was, of course, free to invite Eckert if he felt he needed him. But Major Eckert must have sensed his boss's disapproval. He told his commander in chief that he had too much work to do at the War Department and asked to be excused. Lincoln told him not to give it another thought.

Back at the White House by 11:00 A.M., Lincoln met as scheduled with his cabinet officers. He told the men that he hoped the Confederate leaders would be allowed to return home. He desired no long trials or jail sentences that would continue to divide Americans.

At last, General Grant arrived. Lincoln and the cabinet

secretaries welcomed him enthusiastically and asked him to tell the story of Lee's surrender. That done, they turned their attention to Reconstruction. Everyone seemed to have a different idea about how the conquered South should be treated. Some had written out their ideas for the president to consider. Lincoln listened for a while, then said he did not have time to make any decisions that day. He would read their proposals carefully the next day. One thing was certain, he said. He wanted "no bloody work."

Never So Cheerful

After the cabinet meeting, Grant asked if he might talk to the president privately about a personal matter. He was terribly sorry, but he could not go to the theater with the Lincolns that night. He and Mrs. Grant wanted to go right to New Jersey, where their children were waiting for them. They had been separated for far too long.

There was also another reason, one that Grant did not bring up. His wife simply did not like Mrs. Lincoln. She thought that Mary often behaved more like a queen than a first lady. Only a few weeks earlier, Mary Lincoln had shouted hysterically at her husband on a visit to Union army headquarters. As Mrs. Grant looked on, Mary flew into a jealous rage when she saw the president riding horseback alongside another woman. The episode had deeply embarrassed Mrs. Grant, and she preferred not to see Mrs. Lincoln again.

The president said that he understood, but he must have wondered, did no one want to join him at the theater that night?

Lincoln did not want Grant to feel unappreciated, so the two took a short carriage ride together. Wherever they rode, people cheered them and waved handkerchiefs.

When Lincoln returned to the White House, his workday was far from over. As usual, he had little time for lunch. Typically, he ate only an apple at his desk, peeling and slicing it with his penknife. That afternoon, however, he took a brief meal with Mrs. Lincoln in their private parlor. Afterward, he carried an apple back to his office and turned wearily to the huge pile of requests that covered his desk. These letters came from Union soldiers and their families. Each day, he had to read their pleas and decide whether to punish or pardon them for misbehavior, desertion, or cowardice. Some of their stories broke his heart. More often than not, he allowed such men to go unpunished.

After what seemed like hours, Lincoln decided that he had spent enough time in his office. He had promised his wife that they would take an afternoon carriage ride, and he did not want to disappoint her. At 3:00 P.M., he was finally ready to go. Mary asked her husband if he would like to take anyone else with them. "No," he replied, "I prefer to ride by ourselves to day."

The couple happily rode off together in an open carriage a few minutes later. "I never saw him so supremely cheerful," Mary would later recall. "His manner was even playful. He was so gay, that I said to him, laughingly, 'Dear Husband, you almost startle me by your great cheerfulness. I have not seen you so happy since before Willie's death.'"

"Well I may feel so, Mary," Lincoln answered. "We must *both,* be more cheerful in the future—between the war & the loss of our darling Willie—we have both, been very miserable."

On they rode through Washington on that beautiful spring day. They stopped at one of the president's favorite spots, the Washington Navy Yard, to see the Union ironclad warships that had come back to port after being damaged at the Battle of Fort Fisher.

On their way home, the Lincolns chatted happily about the future. Although his second term as president had begun just six weeks earlier, he dreamed of the day when they might retire. Perhaps they could visit California and see the Rocky Mountains. Or they might go to the Holy Land; Lincoln had always yearned to see Jerusalem. But even if they saved his presidential salary, he said, they would not have enough to live on. He would open a law office back in Springfield, or perhaps in Chicago. He was full of life recalled a friend who knew the Lincolns well. The president spoke about "his little brown cottage, the law office, the court room," happily remembering the days before the war.

Then it was back to the War Department to check the telegraph messages from North Carolina one more time. Any news from General Sherman? None. Lincoln returned to the White House. There was time for yet another meeting, with his old friends from Illinois Isham Haynie and Richard Oglesby. Lincoln took them to the White House reception room and read aloud to them from one of his favorite joke books. No one laughed louder than Lincoln himself.

But evening was approaching. It was time to return to the family quarters and get ready for the theater. Lincoln was pleased to learn that a lovely young couple had agreed to join them as guests in their private box: Clara

Major Henry Rathbone and Clara Harris were sitting with the Lincolns in their box at Ford's Theatre when John Wilkes Booth shot the president. Booth stabbed Rathbone during the struggle.

Harris, daughter of the senator from New York, and her fiancé, Major Henry Rathbone.

Booth Prepares to Kill

By the end of the day, John Wilkes Booth had assigned bloody tasks to his coconspirators. Lewis Powell would kill Secretary of State Seward. George Atzerodt would take care of Vice President Johnson. And Booth, of course, would assassinate the president. Meeting one last time, they agreed on when and where each of them would strike. Booth's old gang was now smaller in number. John H. Surratt had left for Elmira, New York. And although

Samuel Arnold and Michael O'Laughlen, Booth's oldest friends, had been prepared to help Booth kidnap Lincoln, they wanted no part of murder. Neither did Atzerodt, but Booth warned him that he was already named in Booth's letter to the newspapers. It was too late to back out.

Booth was as confident as ever. Earlier in the day, while riding his rented horse along the streets of Washington, he had passed a carriage carrying the Grants and their baggage to the train station. At once recognizing the Union hero, Booth abruptly turned his horse around, pulled alongside Grant's carriage, and "glared" angrily at the general, as his wife later remembered. She thought the "dark, pale man" looked quite "disagreeable."

At 6:00 P.M., Booth returned to Ford's Theatre to prepare for his attack. He stole up to the hallway outside the presidential box on the balcony level. Harry Ford had already prepared the box for Lincoln's arrival. He had removed a wooden wall that separated it from the box next door, so that the Lincolns would have more room. A comfortable rocking chair with red cushions had been brought up from the theater manager's office and placed toward the front of the box for the president. A small, black cane chair had been placed next to it for Mrs. Lincoln. Slightly to the rear was a chair for Miss Harris and a sofa for Major Rathbone. Ford even had borrowed some flags from the Treasury Department to decorate the box.

All was quiet now. The actors had finished their rehearsal and were out having dinner. Booth closed the door of the private hallway behind him. He took out his penknife and began gouging out a hole in the wall opposite the door. Then he put one end of a large stick in the hole

Actress Laura Keene was starring in the play Lincoln was watching when he was shot. Keene was one of the most popular stage personalities of the day. This print shows her about ten years before the Ford's Theatre tragedy.

and the other end against the inside of the door. It fit perfectly. If he wedged it into place later that night before sneaking through the second door leading into the box, no one would be able to enter the hallway after the shooting. Booth placed the stick in a dark corner where no one would see it. Then he cleaned up the pieces of paint and plaster from the floor and left.

At 9:00 P.M., Booth rode his horse into the back alley behind Ford's Theatre. He handed the reins to an old family friend, Edman "Ned" Spangler, who worked there as a stagehand. Spangler had work to do inside, however, so he gave the horse to another theater worker named "Peanuts" John Burroughs. For more than an hour, "Peanuts" clutched the reins of the horse, waiting for Booth to return. He had no idea what the actor was planning to do inside.

Meanwhile, Booth entered the theater from the back and crawled down a trapdoor into its small, dirt-floor cellar. Quietly, he crept under the stage to the other side of the

This is the rocking chair in which Lincoln was sitting at Ford's Theatre the night of April 14, 1865.

building. There he walked back up to street level, brushed off his clothes, and headed next door to Taltavul's saloon.

There was nothing to do now but wait. Booth sat down and ordered a whiskey. Some witnesses later remembered that someone at the bar recognized him. The tipsy stranger called out, "You will never be the actor your father was!"

Booth smirked and calmly answered, "'When I leave the stage, I will be the most talked about man in America.'"

Last Hours Alive

The Lincolns usually took their dinner—if the president had time to sit down to dine at all—at 7:00 P.M. That night, they ate an hour earlier, at 6:00. They wanted to leave plenty of time to get to the theater before the play began. Lincoln seemed to Mary "like a boy out of school" but he also seemed weary. Mary assured him that the play was just the thing he needed to make him forget his cares. She knew how he loved the theater, and so did she. She very much wanted to go that night, too.

But the president's workday just would not end. Before they could leave the White House, Lincoln had yet another meeting, with newspaper reporter Noah Brooks. In a private moment, Lincoln told Brooks that he wished he could stay home and send the reporter to the theater with Mrs. Lincoln instead. But the president realized that his appearance had already been reported in the newspapers. "It has been advertised that we will be there, and I cannot disappoint the people," he told his bodyguard, William H. Crook. "Otherwise I would not go." The truth was, as Mary Lincoln later recalled, "his mind was fixed upon having some relaxation & bent on the theater."

Lincoln dressed himself in his usual formal black suit, white shirt, black bow tie, black vest, and size 14 boots. He placed his gold watch in his vest pocket and arranged the beautiful gold chain. He had won the watch as a prize for donating the most valuable item to a charity event in Chicago. The item he had donated was the original Emancipation Proclamation.

He loaded his coat pockets with other essentials, including his gold-rimmed reading glasses. He had recently broken them but had repaired them himself with a tiny piece of string. He decided to take a second pair of glasses as well, folded inside a leather case. He added a white linen handkerchief on which was sewn in red thread "A. Lincoln." Finally, he added an ivory-handled pocketknife— perhaps the very one he had used earlier in the day to peel his lunchtime apple.

He brought along his wallet, too. It held several

Lincoln stuffed his pockets with these items before leaving for the theater on the night he was assassinated. Included were a small pocketknife, two pairs of glasses, his wallet, a handkerchief, and a Confederate five-dollar bill, among other things. Later, they were found inside his clothing. Today they are preserved at the Library of Congress in Washington, D.C.

well-worn newspaper articles that said good things about him. Many newspapers had been cruel to him during the war; why not save the stories that praised him? His wallet also had a compartment for "U.S. currency," but he carried no American money at all—only a worthless Confederate five-dollar bill, perhaps picked up as a souvenir during his visit to Richmond two weeks earlier.

Mrs. Lincoln wore a light gray, floral print silk dress. She always dressed magnificently, though many people believed that she paid too much attention to her clothes.

As usual, she had picked out the perfect outfit for an evening at the theater.

The weather outside had turned foggy and chilly, so Lincoln brought along the white gloves he hated to wear and a new black overcoat. This was no ordinary coat, but a beautifully designed gift from the New York tailors Brooks Brothers. Lincoln had worn it on inauguration day. Inside the black silk lining were embroidered eagles and the words "One Country, One Destiny."

Lincoln reached for his black stovepipe hat and headed downstairs. One of his aides asked him if he might autograph a photo. "Certainly," Lincoln replied pleasantly, then took a pen and wrote "A. Lincoln" on the small picture.

On the ground floor of the White House, bodyguard Crook was waiting. Did the president want him to come along? No, Lincoln replied, it was not necessary. "You have had a long hard day's work already and must go home to sleep and rest. I cannot afford to have you get all tired out and exhausted."

Every other night, the president used the same words when he left his bodyguard: "Good night, Crook." That night, for some reason, the bodyguard thought he heard Lincoln say, "Goodbye, Crook." For years, Crook wondered why Lincoln had used that phrase. It haunted him for the rest of his life.

On his way out, the president stopped in Robert's bedroom and asked whether his son wanted to join them. Robert said that he was too tired. "All right, my boy," Lincoln replied. "Do just what you feel most like. Good-night."

The Lincolns were already late, but the visitors kept coming. Lincoln had to spend a few minutes more with Speaker of the House Colfax, who returned for his second meeting of the day. There were still more guests to greet, right up to the time he climbed into the waiting carriage. And just as they were about to pull out of the driveway, an old friend arrived. Illinois congressman Isaac N. Arnold asked for just a few minutes of the president's time. Lincoln begged to be excused. "I am going to the theatre," he explained. "Come and see me in the morning."

Congressman George Ashmun wanted a word with Lincoln, too, but instead the president quickly scribbled a pass for Ashmun to use the following morning: "Allow Mr. Ashmun & friend to come in at 9 A.M. to-morrow. A. Lincoln. April 14, 1865." Those were the last words that Lincoln ever wrote.

On to Ford's Theatre

At long last, the carriage lurched forward, hurrying through the bumpy, cobblestone streets to Fifteenth and H Streets, Senator Harris's house. There they picked up Clara Harris and Major Rathbone, then sped off to Tenth and F Streets, the site of Ford's Theatre. It was not a very good neighborhood, but that night there were plenty of people about. Some were marching with torchlights to celebrate the return of peace. The sounds of laughter and singing filled the streets.

The play had been delayed for a few minutes when the president had failed to arrive, but the huge audience had grown restless, and finally the curtain had gone up. The first act was well under way when President and Mrs. Lincoln finally arrived.

Escorted by a White House aide named Charles

Forbes and a police guard named John F. Parker, the Lincolns entered from the back of the audience, then climbed the steps that led up to the balcony. To get to their seats, they had to walk all around the balcony level in a sweeping half circle to reach the right-hand box. A few theatergoers instantly recognized the president and began to applaud. The actors looked up from the stage, caught sight of Lincoln, and stopped in midsentence, joining the ovation. Then the orchestra began to play "Hail to the Chief" in his honor. By the time the Lincolns opened the door that led into their box, the entire audience was cheering. The uproar was "deafening," recalled a man who was there that night. When Lincoln reached his chair, he looked out into the audience and bowed. To one young man in the audience, the president never looked "more happy." As the applause continued, Parker and Forbes took seats outside the outer hallway door.

The play then resumed, and soon Lincoln was laughing at the comedy along with the rest of the audience. Every so often, the actors would surprise everyone by adding Lincoln's name to the script, making the audience roar even loader. Lincoln "laughed heartily and bowed frequently" to the crowd from his seat. Occasionally, the president could be seen peering out into the audience from behind the American flags that draped his box. It was as if he were searching for someone he knew.

At one point, Lincoln reached for Mary's hand and held it tightly. "What will Miss Harris think of my hanging on to you so [?]" Mary asked.

Smiling, her husband answered, "She wont think any thing about it."

"The President Is Shot!"

An intermission followed act 2. The Lincolns remained in their box, chatting with their guests. Parker left his chair outside the hallway and went to Taltavul's saloon for a drink. Unfortunately, he never returned to his post. The door to the hallway leading to the president's box was now unlocked and unguarded except for the White House aide. The theater slowly dimmed its lights, and act 3 was about to begin.

By then, Booth had left the bar. He walked outside onto Tenth Street, then hurried into Ford's Theatre, a black felt hat covering his curly hair. Hidden inside his black suit was a long, sharp knife in a leather case, along with a small pistol that could fire one large bullet. Quietly, Booth crept up the stairs to the balcony, taking the same route that Lincoln had taken earlier in the evening. Few people recognized the latecomer; the eyes of the audience were fixed on the stage.

Booth walked around the back of the balcony, heading for the right-hand box where Lincoln sat. He had expected to find a policeman or soldier on guard and was surprised to see no one to block his way. The only one outside the hallway door was Forbes. Booth boldly handed Forbes his card. Forbes looked at it. Here was the famous actor John Wilkes Booth! Forbes was only too happy to let him pass.

Opening the door, Booth slid into the hallway leading to the private boxes. The wooden stick was exactly where he had left it. Trying not to make a sound, he placed one end in the hole he had carved in the wall and pressed the other end against the door. No one else would be able to enter.

This is the pistol that John Wilkes Booth used to shoot Lincoln. The murderer held the small gun only a few inches from the back of the president's head.

Booth could hear the muffled voices of the actors onstage below. He peered into a tiny hole in the inner door to box 7—Lincoln's box. The theater owner had drilled the hole long before that night so that he could keep close watch whenever important guests sat inside. Now Booth used it to see where his target was sitting. There, right before his eyes, sat Abraham Lincoln, at Booth's mercy at last.

Booth could easily make out the president, holding his wife's hand. His back was to Booth. With one hand, Booth took his pistol from his pocket. With the other, he clutched the handle on the inner door, waiting. It was around 10:13 P.M.

On the gaslit stage below, actors Laura Keene, Harry Hawk, and Helen Muzzy were exchanging funny lines. "Don't know the manners of good society, eh?" shouted Hawk. As the two actresses left the stage, Hawk yelled after them, "Well, I guess I know enough to turn you inside

The presidential box at Ford's Theatre as it looked the day after the assassination. The draped flag is still torn from Booth's spur.

out, old gal—you sockdologizing old man-trap." The audience laughed loudly, just as Booth knew they would. Lincoln joined the merriment. As he did, Booth opened the inner door and stepped forward into the box. In an instant, he aimed his pistol directly behind the president's head and pulled the trigger, sending a bullet slicing through Lincoln's brain.

The noise exploded in the theater, startling the crowd. Foul-smelling smoke rose from the president's box. For a moment, Hawk froze in his place. No one in the audience moved. Was this part of the play? "You could have heard a pin drop," recalled one actor who was waiting in the wings to go on.

The Murder Scene

No artists or photographers were on hand to witness the shooting of Lincoln at Ford's Theatre on April 14, 1865. But so many Americans were eager to see pictures of the murder that artists had to create images out of their imaginations. Some did well. The famous printmakers Currier & Ives of New York showed Booth attacking Lincoln from behind and Major Henry Rathbone rising to try to stop the assassin *(below)*. But Lincoln was not clutching an American flag when he was shot. Other prints *(opposite)* showed the president sitting in the wrong part of his theater box or depicted an extra person in the president's party. Perhaps the most ridiculous showed Lincoln standing up after the shooting and holding his bleeding head, while musicians waved their instruments at Booth *(opposite, bottom)*. Picture buyers were so hungry for these scenes that they bought almost anything that was printed.

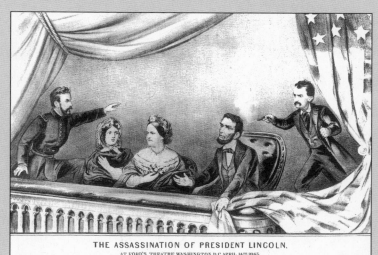

THE ASSASSINATION OF PRESIDENT LINCOLN,
AT FORD'S THEATRE WASHINGTON, D.C. APRIL 14TH 1865.

Back up in the box, Major Rathbone saw Lincoln slump over in his chair. Then, through the smoke, he glimpsed the stranger behind him. Realizing what had happened, Rathbone leaped to his feet, darting toward the intruder. Booth quickly threw down his gun and took out the large knife. Yelling something that sounded like "The south is avenged!" he lunged at Rathbone, stabbing him viciously in the arm and sending blood spurting everywhere.

Then Booth reached for the railing of the box, climbed over the edge, and leaped down to the stage below. It was a twelve-foot jump. Booth had made many such leaps as an actor; in fact, he was famous for them. But this time, Rathbone grabbed desperately for Booth's coat, and Booth tumbled down clumsily, catching the spur of his boot on the flag draped beneath the box. He landed hard and off balance on the stage, breaking his left leg as he hit the wooden floor. Even with the pain ripping through his leg, he managed to stand up for all the audience to see, bloody knife still in his hand, and shouted the Latin motto of the state of Virginia: "Sic Semper Tyrannis!" (Thus Ever to Tyrants). To the orchestra leader standing in shock only a few feet away, Booth looked like "a wild beast."

As Booth limped across the stage toward the wings, Rathbone shouted, "Stop that man!" Mary Lincoln, cradling her unconscious husband to keep him from falling over, caught her breath and suddenly filled the air with loud shrieks. "Murder!" she shouted over and over. "Murder!"

Finally, someone in the stunned crowd realized what had happened and cried, "The President is shot!" As Booth fled from view, others screamed, "Catch him!" "Hang him!" "Kill him!" But Booth had already disappeared from sight.

In a split second, panic filled the theater. The curtain

came down suddenly. Men rushed into the aisles, turning over their chairs and smashing them under their feet. Women fainted. The mad scene, one of the actresses remembered, was like "the hell of hells." Someone shouted for a doctor.

Dr. Charles A. Leale was sitting in the Ford's Theatre balcony when John Wilkes Booth shot Lincoln. He was the first doctor to reach the scene and immediately knew that Lincoln would die. He had graduated from medical college only two months earlier.

As screams continued echoing through the theater, people from the balcony tried desperately to open the blockaded door leading to Lincoln's box. They pounded and pushed but could not budge it. Booth's wedge held fast. Finally, drenched in blood, Rathbone managed to push aside the stick, and the door flew open. A crowd surged inside, but Rathbone, badly wounded and still bleeding, begged that only doctors be allowed to come in.

The first medical man on the scene was a twenty-three-year-old army surgeon named Charles A. Leale, who had been sitting nearby in the balcony. Entering the box, Leale found Lincoln still sitting in his rocking chair and Mary trying desperately to keep his head from falling over to the right.

"Oh, Doctor, is he dead?" cried Mary as Leale rushed to examine the president. "Can he recover? Do what you can for him. Oh, my dear husband." The young doctor replied that he would do all he could. Mary soon dissolved into bitter tears.

Leale felt for a pulse on the president's cold, damp wrist. Finding none, he and a few other men lifted him from his chair, cutting open his coat and shirt to search for knife or bullet wounds. None could be found.

Two other doctors, Albert King and Charles Sabin Taft, now rushed to the scene. Some men lifted Taft up from the stage level; others grabbed his arms from above and hoisted him inside the box. The doctors tenderly placed Lincoln on the floor, with Mrs. Lincoln wailing nearby. Leale forced open Lincoln's eyes. His pupils were rolled back. The doctor understood at once that the president had suffered a brain injury.

Leale ran his hand through the thick hair on the back of Lincoln's head until he found the wound. He stuck his finger into the bullet hole and dug out the clot of blood that had already covered it. He then began massaging the president's heart. Bending over the president's body, Leale placed his mouth over Lincoln's and began blowing air into his lungs in a desperate effort to revive him.

At last, Lincoln's heart began beating again. Leale again checked his pulse and listened for his breath. Lincoln was breathing on his own. Someone passed up some brandy, and Leale poured a few drops into Lincoln's mouth. But Leale knew that Lincoln would never wake up. He could do nothing to help. Leale looked up and said, "His wound is mortal. It is impossible for him to recover."

In the chaos, others pushed forward into the box. Actress Laura Keene, horrified by what had happened, begged only to be allowed to cradle the president's head in her lap for a few minutes. By the time she left, her costume was spattered with blood. It was not Lincoln's blood, however, but poor Rathbone's. Everyone was paying attention to Lincoln, and no one seemed to notice that the major was still bleeding badly.

All was confusion, but everyone agreed that the president must not be allowed to end his life here. He must be taken from the theater and placed somewhere to die in dignity and comfort. But try as they might, the men inside the box could not push back the crowd that had pressed forward to view the terrible scene. "Guards clear the passage!" Leale shouted. Drawing their swords, some soldiers on the scene forced the people back all the way to the exits.

In all the confusion and horror, no one is sure how Lincoln was carried from Ford's Theatre. Some remembered that he was lifted tenderly by several men, headfirst, with Mrs. Lincoln following and sobbing. Others remembered that the small, portable wall lying in the state box was used as a stretcher. Still others said that a shutter was ripped from one of the windows and brought inside so that Lincoln could be placed on it. One witness even swore that the president was carried out in his rocking chair.

One way or the other, the men managed to get the president slowly downstairs and out the front door. But they were not at all sure what to do next. Someone suggested that he be brought back to the White House. No, Leale said, such a long trip, sitting up in a carriage over bumpy roads, would kill him quickly.

"Bring him in here, bring him in here!" someone shouted from a small building across the street. This was the tailor William Petersen's house. The rooms upstairs were rented to boarders. The president was carried up the winding staircase that led to the front door, lifted inside, and placed on a small bed in the tiny bedroom at the rear of the house.

Back in the street, a parade of marchers out celebrating the end of the war came to a sudden halt in confusion outside the theater. At first no one was quite sure what was happening, but the news spread quickly. President Lincoln had been shot inside the theater. Now he lay dying in the humble boarding house across the way.

Booth Flees; Seward Survives

While all this was happening at Ford's Theatre, Lewis Powell appeared at Secretary of State Seward's door, pretending he had medicine to deliver. When Seward's son Frederick tried to block the way, Powell aimed his gun at

The house where Lincoln died. Doctors were afraid to take the wounded president along the bumpy roads to the White House. This boarding house was just across the street from Ford's Theatre.

him and pulled the trigger. For some reason, the gun did not fire. Powell took the gun by the barrel and brought it crashing down on Frederick's head, sending him sprawling to the floor. Then Powell took out his knife, rushed upstairs, and began stabbing Seward as he lay in his bed.

Because of his carriage-accident injuries, Seward was wearing an iron brace around his neck. The brace saved his life. Strong as he was, Powell was unable to stab through the metal. Seward's face was badly cut and was scarred for life, but he survived. Powell fled the house, screaming, "I'm mad! I'm mad!"

George Atzerodt did not even try to kill Vice President Johnson. He was too frightened and probably too drunk. Instead, he went to a cousin's house in Maryland and hid there. Five days later, he would be captured.

Despite a "burning" pain in his badly broken leg, Booth somehow managed to limp to the back of the theater. Reaching the back alley, he grabbed his horse, hit poor "Peanuts" Burroughs over the head with the handle of his knife, mounted up, and galloped away while screams from inside filled the air. He was on his way to the river bridge that led into southern Maryland by the time the president was placed on the bed where he would spend his final hours.

Booth Wanted Them Killed, Too

President Lincoln was not the only target of Booth's gang of assassins on April 14, 1865. Secretary of State William H. Seward of New York (1801–1872) was attacked that night by Lewis Powell but survived his wounds. Vice President Andrew Johnson (1808–1875) was targeted for death, too, but the man assigned to kill him lost his nerve and instead ran away. Johnson became president the day Lincoln died, and Seward remained at the State Department for four more years.

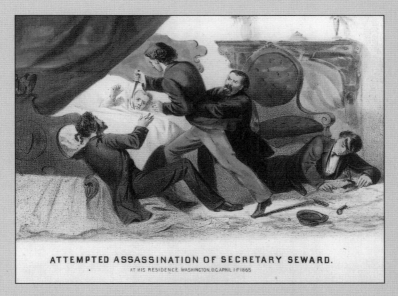

ATTEMPTED ASSASSINATION OF SECRETARY SEWARD.
AT HIS RESIDENCE, WASHINGTON, D.C. APRIL 14 1865

Lewis Powell stabbed William H. Seward in his bedroom on April 14, 1865. Seward's iron neck brace saved his life.

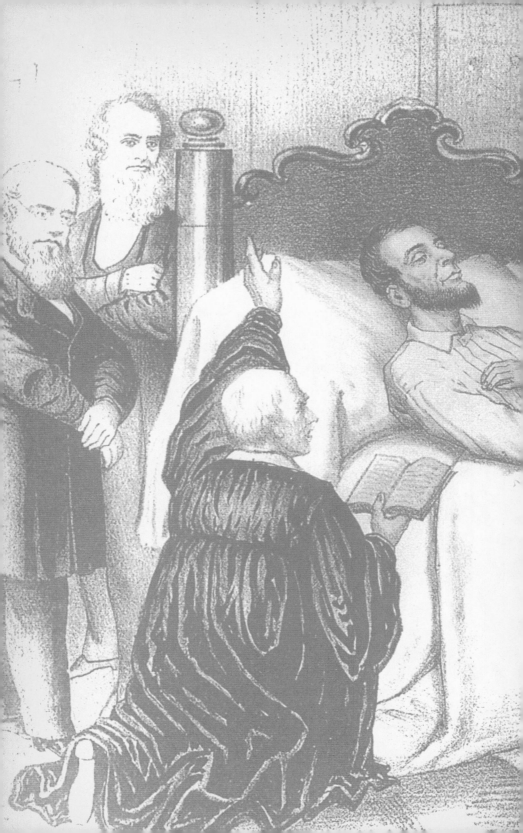

Chapter Five

April 15, 1865

While John Wilkes Booth was quickly escaping, Abraham Lincoln was slowly dying.

Stretched out across the small bed in the back bedroom of the Petersen House, his head propped up on two pillows, the president's eyes remained closed, his breathing faint. Earlier, doctors had removed his clothing to search for other wounds. They found none but could not help admiring Lincoln's strong chest and bulging arm muscles. Like most Americans, the doctors had heard stories about his legendary strength. Now they knew that those stories were true.

Lincoln's Final Hours

Dr. Charles Leale felt Lincoln's hands and feet. They were cold. The doctor ordered hot-water bottles and heated blankets to keep the president warm. Downstairs in the Petersens' kitchen, mustard and flour were boiled into a paste—a mustard plaster, it was called. It was brought up in steaming pots to be spread over Lincoln's chest and legs like thick clay. Even so, his body remained icy.

The surgeon general of the United States, Joseph Barnes, was summoned to Lincoln's bedside. The Lincolns' family doctor, Robert King Stone, arrived as well. Neither could do anything further to help the patient.

Mary Lincoln grew more hysterical by the hour. Bending over the bed, she kissed her husband's face over and over, begging him to speak to her. "Why didn't he shoot me?" she pleaded. An onlooker would never forget the "pitiful picture" of Mrs. Lincoln, "insane with . . . agony, moaning and sobbing" throughout "that terrible night." Finally, Mary was led away to lie down on a sofa in the front parlor. "Oh, shoot me, Doctor," she cried. "Why don't you shoot me, too?"

Laura Keene, the star of *Our American Cousin*, pushed her way across the street from the theater to pay her respects. Her dress was still spattered with blood from her earlier visit to the president's box.

Major Henry Rathbone, clutching the arm into which Booth had plunged his dagger, stayed at the boarding house as long as he could. He soon fainted, however, and was taken home and put to bed.

As soon as Secretary of War Stanton heard the news of the shooting, he raced to the Petersen house. When he entered, he found the president near death and the first lady sobbing uncontrollably. Stanton asked the doctors for a report on Lincoln's condition. They informed him that Lincoln would not live much longer.

Stanton quickly took charge. While the doctors worked on Lincoln in the next room, he took over the rear parlor and began asking questions. Stanton interviewed people who had witnessed the crime. By 1:30 A.M., he was certain that the shot had been fired by Booth. Word raced out on telegraph wires that the president had been attacked. The order went out to protect all Union forts and arrest all suspicious men. If Stanton could help it, he would not let the South start the war again.

Booth Gallops South

While the president lay unconscious inside Ford's Theatre, Booth was galloping south toward the Navy Yard Bridge, which led across a small branch of the Potomac River and out of Washington. He was not alone for long.

Davy Herold, a member of Booth's gang, was soon riding after him. Herold had been told to wait outside Secretary of State Seward's home while Lewis Powell attacked him. But Herold had been frightened by the bloodcurdling screams he heard coming from the house. Leaving Powell behind, he mounted his horse and fled to meet Booth.

Even though the war was all but over, a soldier still guarded the Navy Yard Bridge. When Booth rode up to his post, the guard asked who he was and where he was

The Deathbed

Abraham Lincoln died in the tiny back bedroom of a modest boarding house, but many artists thought that such a setting was not good enough for the beloved president. Besides, many famous visitors had come to the scene briefly to say goodbye during the night, and all of them needed to be shown. So the artists made the bedroom look much bigger than it was, in some cases big enough to be in a royal palace. Most picture makers also showed Mary Lincoln at the scene, even though she was not at her husband's bedside when he took his last breath. Many also showed Vice President Andrew Johnson on hand. In truth, his visit had been very brief because Mary hated him so. Later, she would tell a friend that she thought he had been part of the plot to kill her husband. Even so, Americans wanted to see the new president and the dying president together, perhaps to show viewers that the country would go on.

This exaggerated scene made the tiny Petersen House chamber swell to the size of a palace ballroom.

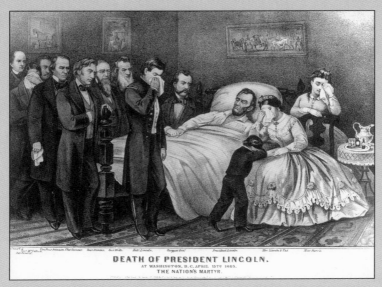

Currier & Ives's scene includes son Tad, who never visited the death scene.

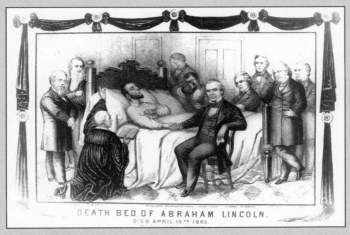

A minister prays while Vice President Johnson holds Lincoln's hand in this ridiculous scene. Mary is in the background kissing her son Robert.

headed. The bold assassin did not try to hide his identity. He told them his name and said only that he was heading home to Beantown, Maryland. Unaware that Lincoln had just been shot, the soldier let Booth pass, and on he galloped across the river. A few minutes later, Herold followed. He, too, was allowed to cross after telling the guard a fake story about searching for a woman.

Shortly before midnight, Booth and Herold met up about eight miles into southern Maryland. Then they galloped off together, as planned, toward the Surratt tavern. "I . . . rode sixty miles that night," Booth later exaggerated, "with the bones of my leg tearing the flesh at every jump." Around midnight, they pounded on the tavern door. Booth drank some whiskey and picked up the binoculars brought there by Mary Surratt. His broken leg was causing him so much pain that he could not even carry the gun that was waiting for him.

Pain or not, Booth knew that he had to press on. Farther and farther he rode, with Herold at his side. They reached a little village known only as T.B. between 1:00 and 2:00 A.M., and from there galloped to the farmhouse of Dr. Samuel Mudd, near the Maryland village of Bryantown. The assassin was desperate for medical attention.

Booth reached the Mudd home at about 4:00 A.M. Aroused from his bed, the doctor examined Booth's leg and told him that it was badly fractured. Mudd took two thin pieces of wood from a hatbox and made a splint for him. Then he gave Booth crutches and some food and invited him to rest there for as long as he could.

For years thereafter, Mudd insisted that he did not recognize Booth that night and had played no part in the assassination plot. Booth wore a fake beard, he claimed. He did not know him that well to begin with, and as a doctor, he had no choice but to help an injured man. But most experts on the Lincoln murder strongly believe that Mudd was involved in Booth's kidnapping plan from the beginning. That meant he also was responsible when the kidnapping plot became a murder plot. A court would later agree.

The Death Watch

Like his father, eleven-year-old Tad Lincoln went to the theater on the night of April 14—but to Grover's Theater, not Ford's. While he was happily watching the play *Aladdin*, a messenger arrived from the White House and whispered the horrifying news into the ear of the man who had brought the president's son. Quickly, they led Tad from the theater and took him home. Some people in the audience thought that they heard the boy screaming as he left the theater. Once Tad was gone, the managers stopped the play and told the audience about the shooting.

Robert Lincoln got the awful news before Tad reached home. Along with John Hay, one of Lincoln's private secretaries, he raced to the Petersen house to comfort his mother and visit the bedside. Overcome by the sight of his father so still and pale, he began to sob, but then he got control of his grief. When his mother started to wail again, Robert squeezed her hand and begged, "Mother, please put your trust in God and all will be well." Mrs. Lincoln could not do so.

Other members of the cabinet began arriving. They took turns visiting their chief's bedside and trying to pay their respects to Mrs. Lincoln. From time to time, they held official meetings inside the Petersen house with Stanton, nervously planning what to do next. Seward, they learned, might be dying, too. Where was Vice President Johnson? Who would be attacked next? "Damn the Rebels," cursed Secretary of the Navy Gideon Welles. "This is their work!"

Welles later described the sad form of Lincoln lying on his deathbed:

> The giant sufferer . . . had been stripped of his clothes. His large arms, which were occasionally exposed, were of a size which one would scarce have expected from his spare appearance. His slow, full respiration lifted the clothes with each breath that he took. His features were calm and striking.

Vice President Johnson finally arrived around 2:00 A.M. He looked as if he had been drinking and stayed only a short time. He knew that Mary Lincoln disliked him, and he did not want to upset her further.

On through the night and into the morning, Lincoln's family and friends watched, waited, and wept. Eventually, Lincoln's breathing became louder and more strained. The doctors tried sticking long needles into his wound to find the bullet and remove it, but they failed. It was lodged too deeply inside his brain. No more treatments were attempted. The doctors simply tried to make Lincoln's final hours as comfortable as possible.

Dr. Leale held tightly to Lincoln's hand. In case the President could feel anything at all, Leale wanted him to know that he had a friend nearby. But Lincoln never stirred, and soon his right eye began to swell and turn black.

Toward 3:00 A.M., Mary made another visit to her husband's bedside. Before she entered the room, a clean white napkin was placed on the president's pillow to hide the blood still oozing from the back of his head. Mary dissolved into sobs that "brought tears to every eye."

By early morning, the newspapers were already reporting the "highly important" news. The streets of Washington filled with confused, anxious citizens. No one seemed to know where to go or what to do next. Most people wept openly. Others voiced their anger, vowing to

Harper's Weekly, *a popular illustrated newspaper, featured the first picture of the assassination. Thousands of readers saw it.*

kill Booth and all rebels. When one foolish man shouted into a crowd that he was glad Booth had fired his gun at Lincoln, a soldier shot and killed him. When another yelled, "Long live Jefferson Davis," an angry mob nearly tore him to pieces.

Many of the president's admirers began gathering outside the Petersen house, filling Tenth Street. Each time a dignitary left the building, the crowd begged for news about the president.

At 6:00 A.M., a gentle rain began to fall in Washington. Lincoln was now gasping for air. After each breath came a long pause, then a rattling noise and what sounded almost like a sigh. Robert cried quietly on the shoulder of Senator Charles Sumner.

Reverend Phineas Gurley, the minister of the church the Lincolns often attended, was now in the room as well. Standing by the bed, he prayed silently. The tiny room could hold only a few people at a time, so the well-wishers, friends, and family had to take turns visiting. From the front parlor, Mary could be heard moaning. Earlier, she had begged Robert to send for Taddie. She was sure her husband would wake up if only he could hear the child's voice, for "he loved him so well." Robert gently told her that Tad must be kept away; he could do his father no good now.

When 6:30 came, doctors noted that Lincoln's breathing was "jerking." He was still drawing breath but "at long pauses." Around 7:00, the doctors asked Mary if she wanted to visit the bedside again—perhaps for the last time. When she entered the room and saw how awful her husband looked, she fainted to the floor. Doctors helped awaken her and tenderly led her toward the president.

She tried desperately to speak to her husband. "Love," she pleaded, "live but one moment to speak to our children!" But all she heard was a frightening grunt and a gasp for air, and once again she melted into tears, groaning and shrieking. Out of patience, Stanton ordered, "Take that woman out and do not let her in again!"

Robert helped her from the room. "Oh, My God," Mary wailed as she left. "And have I given my husband to die!"

The doctors now crowded around the bed, listening closely to the president's last breaths. The room was silent. Dr. Leale placed his finger on Lincoln's pulse. At 7:22 A.M., the great man's heartbeat fluttered and finally stopped. One of the doctors looked up from the bedside and said softly, "He is gone."

Stanton, barely able to speak, asked Reverend Gurley if he would say a prayer. The minister knelt at Lincoln's bedside. As he began to speak, Robert grasped the edge of his father's blanket, and everyone else in the room reached out and touched their hands to the bed, too. Gurley's prayer was brief. "God," he asked, "please accept this good man, Abraham Lincoln, into the kingdom of heaven." Every man in the room whispered, "Amen."

Stanton looked at the dead president. He thought for a moment of the war that Lincoln had fought to save the Union, the slaves he had helped to free, the history he had made. Then he looked up and said to all of the people who had watched Lincoln die, "Now he belongs to the ages."

Not long afterward, a hard rain began to fall outside. Robert carefully led his sobbing mother down the winding staircase that led from the Petersen house to the street, where a carriage waited to take her back to the White House. As she left, Mary lifted her head, looked across the road, and saw before her the theater where her husband had been murdered. "That dreadful house!" she cried. "That dreadful house!"

Fugitive on the Run

By morning, the streets of Washington were filled with posters offering a $100,000 reward for the capture of Booth and his accomplices. "All good citizens," read the printed message from Secretary of War Stanton, were warned to "rest neither night nor day" until the murderers were found.

"Booth is 5 feet 7 or 8 inches high, slender build, high forehead, black hair, black eyes, and wears a heavy black moustache," read the description. Anyone shielding or protecting him faced the sentence of death himself.

Soon Dr. Mudd, out and about in Bryantown, heard a report that Booth had murdered Lincoln and was headed in their direction. Dr. Mudd hurried home. If he had not known at first that Booth had shot Lincoln, he certainly did now.

Before 6:00 P.M., Booth and Herold stole away from the Mudd farmhouse and headed into the swampland nearby. At 9:00 P.M., they turned up at the log cabin of a free black man named Oswell Swann. Booth may have hated black people, but as Mudd probably told him, Swann knew the swamps like the back of his hand and could guide them to safety. Later Mudd would lie to detectives about the direction in which Booth had headed.

Swann led Booth and Herold to the home of a Confederate sympathizer named Samuel Cox, who hid them in the woods near his home on the cliffs above the Potomac River. Other sympathizers brought them food to eat and newspapers to read. The papers were filled with stories about the assassination. Here, at least for a while, they would be safe.

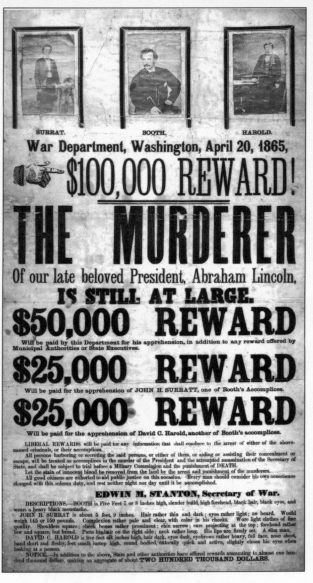

Reward posters appeared in Washington only hours after Lincoln's death. They identified John Wilkes Booth as the assassin. This later edition added photographs of the accused conspirators.

Chapter Six

The Nation Weeps

On the morning of April 15, Andrew Johnson was sworn in as the seventeenth president of the United States. Lincoln had been right: the work of the Union would go on, even if someone managed to kill him.

Not long after Johnson took the oath of office, Lincoln's body was placed in a coffin and driven back to the White House. There, in total secrecy, doctors cut open his head and found the bullet that had taken his life. They even weighed Lincoln's brain. They believed they would find it to be larger and heavier than that of an ordinary man, but it was not. How, then, could they explain his wisdom, his patience? No one had an answer.

The undertakers then prepared Lincoln's body for his funeral. They dressed him in one of his black suits,

This drawing of Lincoln in his coffin was made by artist George Koch in Indianapolis.

cleaned his blood-soaked hair, and applied makeup to his face. The undertakers managed to make Lincoln's features look peaceful, even happy, just as he had appeared on the last day of his life.

Mary Lincoln remained upstairs in her bedroom, the curtains drawn tightly to keep out the light. "The wails of a broken heart" filled the mansion. Little Tad tried in vain to comfort her. "Don't cry so, Mamma!" he pleaded with her. "Don't cry, or you will make me cry, too!" The only other sound in the house was the noise of hammering coming from the carpenters working downstairs. They were busy building a platform to hold the president's coffin in the East Room—just as Lincoln had dreamed in his frightening nightmare only a few weeks before.

Far from Washington, out on the Illinois prairie where Lincoln had once lived, the president's cousin Dennis Hanks heard the news about the assassination. He quickly went to Sarah Bush Lincoln's place to tell her about her stepson.

"Aunt Sairy," Dennis said, "Abe's dead."

"Yes, I know, Denny," the old woman replied. "I knowed they'd kill him. I ben awaiting fur it."

The American Saint

On Easter Sunday, April 16, the Union wept along with Mary Lincoln. The bells tolled. Churches, black ribbons draping their pulpits, overflowed with worshipers. Ministers throughout the North spoke tenderly of the dead president. In their sadness, they compared him to the great heroes of the Bible.

He was like Moses, many of the preachers said. He had led people to freedom, but he had died before he could reach the promised land. Others said that he was like Jesus, who also had been put to death on Good Friday and had died for his people's sins.

They spoke of Lincoln's honesty, kindness, brilliance, and belief in God. One preacher summed it up with great emotion: Lincoln was "something greater than greatness itself." Overnight, Abraham Lincoln had become an American saint in the hearts and minds of many of his countrymen.

Not just Christians felt the loss. That very week, Jews were celebrating Passover. In synagogues throughout the North, congregations heard rabbis speak with great emotion of the dead Lincoln. He was their hero, too.

In the South, the reaction was mixed. "I *can't* be sorry," one Virginia woman said of Lincoln's assassination. "I believe it was the vengeance of the Lord." A Georgia soldier agreed, noting that Lincoln's "tragic death was no more than just punishment for the crime" against the South. But a North Carolina newspaper reported the news with "profound grief," and many southern soldiers expressed their disapproval when they learned that Booth had shot Lincoln from behind.

Black people in the South were deeply saddened. In South Carolina, the African American children at one school took to wearing black ribbons on their clothes.

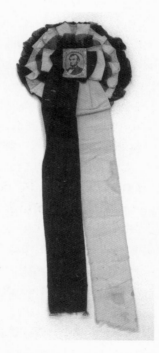

To honor the dead president, mourners pinned ribbons like this one to their clothes. Most featured a picture of Lincoln surrounded by black ribbon.

When that did not seem tribute enough, they made a black wreath and gave it to their teacher.

The newspapers were filled with stories of Lincoln's heroic life and sudden death. Americans read the details hungrily. Many men wore funeral badges on their coats, some with tiny photos of the late president. Women wore black. Poets offered tributes, too. William Cullen Bryant, who had first met Lincoln in 1860, wrote:

> In sorrow by thy bier we stand,
>   Amid the awe that hushes all,
> And speak the anguish of a land
>   That shook with horror at thy fall.
>
> Thy task is done; the bond are free;
>   We bear thee to an honored grave,
> Whose proudest monument shall be
>   The broken fetters of the slave.

Soon northerners began decorating their homes with images and statues of the late hero. Printmakers rushed to produce scenes of the murder and the deathbed. No artist had actually seen either the shooting or Lincoln's final hours, so they based their pictures on newspaper descriptions or in some cases merely made up the details themselves. Some of the prints were ridiculous, showing dozens of people crowded into the tiny room where Lincoln died. But truth did not seem to matter.

Thousands of prints flooded the country. An admirer could buy one for as little as ten cents. Once, Americans had decorated their homes with pictures of religious saints. Now they did so with pictures of Lincoln.

WE CHERISH HIS MEMORY.

A NEATLY PRINTED

Mourning Envelope

With the above excellent Likeness of

OUR BELOVED DEPARTED,

IS NOW READY FOR THE TRADE.

Orders may be sent to S. O. THAYER, over Boylston market, Boston; or to
B. B. RUSSELL & Co., No. 55 Cornhill, Boston.

☞ All orders by Mail, Express, or Telegraph, promptly responded to.

*For months after Lincoln's death, many of his admirers used specially
decorated mourning envelopes like the one advertised here for their mail.*

These pictures became precious to Americans. Before
April 15, 1865, to display a picture of Lincoln meant you
were probably a Republican or a relative of a soldier fighting
for the Union cause. Afterward, Lincoln became a hero to
nearly everyone in the North. His kindly, bearded face
seemed to be everywhere.

Lincoln is welcomed into heaven in this imaginary scene. Most Americans of the day were deeply religious, and many decorated their homes with pictures like this that showed angels escorting the late president.

The Long Journey Home

A private funeral service was held inside the White House on April 19. Robert was the only member of the family who attended the ceremony. Mary remained upstairs with Tad, still too upset to leave her room and appear in public. General Ulysses S. Grant and President Andrew Johnson were there, along with Mrs. Lincoln's sisters. Reverend Phineas Gurley gave the sermon. The land, he said, was "filled with sorrow." After the service, more than six hundred special guests filed by to look at Lincoln lying inside his coffin.

At 2:00 P.M., as thousands looked on silently, the coffin was moved in a slow march up Pennsylvania Avenue to the Capitol. No one planned it, but African American soldiers led the march. Many people crowding the streets thought this a perfect tribute to Lincoln. Hundreds more soldiers and dignitaries marched behind the horse-drawn hearse. Bands played mournful songs, and muffled drums kept beat with the marchers' footsteps.

Only six weeks earlier, Lincoln had been inaugurated at the Capitol. Now his body was placed on a large black

As thousands looked on, Lincoln's funeral procession wound through the streets of Washington on April 19, 1865. The hearse was pulled by six white horses.

A black-draped train carried the president's remains from Washington to Springfield, Illinois.

platform in the Rotunda. For the rest of that afternoon and all through the next day, people waited in long lines for the chance to pay their respects to their fallen leader. Guns fired salutes outside, and just as on inauguration day, the sun burst through the clouds.

Finally, on Thursday, April 20, Lincoln's coffin was taken to a special railroad car for his final trip home. The casket bearing the body of his son Willie, who had died three years earlier, was removed from a Washington cemetery and placed next to that of his father.

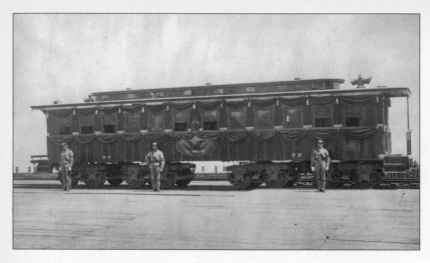

The president's body traveled in this railroad car, guarded by soldiers, during the long journey to Springfield, Illinois.

As the train headed west, it paused for large public funerals at many stops along the way. The first was held in Baltimore on April 21. In the city where Lincoln had once been forced to wear a disguise to escape a murder plot, black crape and pictures of the president now filled shop windows. Ten thousand people walked past his coffin to pay their respects. The scene was repeated in city after city.

As the train slowly rolled through the countryside, people clutching flowers lined up along the tracks to lift their hats, wave, and cry. At night, they lit bonfires along the route. It must have seemed to those on board the train that nearly everyone in America had come to say a personal goodbye.

In Philadelphia, Lincoln's body lay in state at Independence Hall. Four years before, on his way to Washington to become president, he had raised the flag there. He had told the people that he "would rather be assassinated on this spot

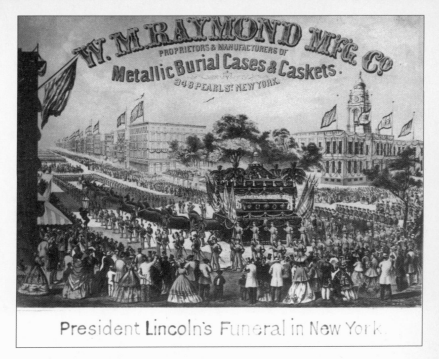

President Lincoln's Funeral in New York.

Lincoln's casket rolls down Broadway during his New York funeral. Local democrats tried to prevent blacks from marching, but the War Department ordered that everyone be allowed to participate.

than to surrender it." He had never had to give up Independence Hall, but he had paid with his life to keep the Union together. Now he was back, and three hundred thousand people pressed to get in to view his body.

The New York City funeral went on for two days, with half a million people taking part. In a solemn parade that lasted for nearly four hours, thousands of marchers followed the coffin down Broadway to City Hall. Inside City Hall, thousands more lined up for the chance to gaze on Lincoln's face one last time. Women tried to kiss him but were held back by guards. One boy somehow managed to place on the body a wreath of flowers in the shape of

The Colored People in the Procession To-day.

WASHINGTON, April 24, 1865.

Major-General JOHN A. DIX—It is the desire of the Secretary of War that no discrimination respecting color should be exercised in admitting persons to the funeral procession to-morrow. In this city a black regiment formed part of the escort.

C. A. DANA, Assistant Secretary of War.

Colored people, or their societies, who wish to join the procession to-day, can do so by forming on West Reade street by twelve o'clock, their right resting on Broadway. Societies should appoint their own Marshals to preserve order.

Special Time Table for Funeral Train, on Hudson River Railroad, to-day, Tuesday, April 25.

Leave NEW YORK, 29th		Leave HYDE PARK, .	7.56, P.M.
street, . . .	4.00, P.M.	STAATSBURG,	8.08, "
MANHATTAN, .	4.20, "	RHINEBECK, .	8.24, "
YONKERS, . .	4.45, "	BARRYTOWN, .	8.40, "
DOBBS' FERRY,	5.00, "	TIVOLI, . .	8.52, "
IRVINGTON, .	5.07, "	GERMANTOWN,	9.10, "
TARRYTOWN, .	5.15, "	CATSKILL, . .	9.27, "
SING SING, . .	5.30, "	Arrive HUDSON, . .	9.38, "
Arrive PEEKSKILL, .	5.57, "	Leave HUDSON, . .	9.41, "
Leave PEEKSKILL, .	6.00, "	STOCKPORT, .	9.52, "
GARRISON'S, .	6.26, "	COXSACKIE, .	10.00, "
COLD SPRING, .	6.33, "	STUYVESANT,	10.07, "
FISHKILL, . .	6.50, "	SCHODACK, .	10.26, "
N. HAMBURG, .	7.06, "	CASTLETON, .	10.35, "
Arrive POUGHKEEPSIE 7.25, "		Arrive EAST ALBANY 10.55, "	
Leave POUGHKEEPSIE 7.40, "			

The government issued special schedules allowing African Americans to march in tribute to their dead leader. But their participation was restricted.

The president's body was placed on view in New York's City Hall on April 24, 1865. Thousands of citizens lined up for the chance to take one last look at Lincoln's face.

THE BODY OF THE MARTYR PRESIDENT, ABRAHAM LINCOLN.
LYING IN STATE AT THE CITY HALL, N.Y., APRIL 24 & 25, 1865.

Lincoln's initials, A.L. Later that day, with the initials still showing on Lincoln's chest, a photographer took a picture of the president lying in his coffin. It was the only photograph of Lincoln in death.

In the days to come, more parades and funerals took place in Albany and Buffalo, New York; Cleveland and Columbus, Ohio; and Indianapolis and Michigan City, Indiana. Tens of thousands of mourners came to look, pray, and weep. Many wore small pictures of Lincoln like badges on their coats and held up large signs paying tribute to him. Thick bouquets of spring flowers crowded open windows and black ribbons could be seen floating from many public buildings.

At the funeral in Cleveland on April 28, 1865, thousands of citizens waited in the rain for the chance to view Lincoln's body.

The Columbus, Ohio, funeral took place on April 29, 1865. Mourners filled the streets with fresh flowers. The horse-drawn hearse rolled over a carpet of roses.

Laid to Rest at Last

Not until Monday morning, May 1, did the funeral train reach Chicago. Here Lincoln had argued many law cases, given important political speeches, and had many good friends. Here, five years before, Republicans had nominated him for president. Now he was back for the last time.

The Chicago funeral rivaled New York's in size and magnificence. Signs read "Tenderly Bear Him to His Rest" and "Snatched from the Cold and Formal World." Marchers followed the body to the county courthouse, where thousands of people waited in long lines for a final look at the man who had risen to greatness among them. Then, at last, Lincoln headed home to Springfield.

While all these solemn tributes were taking place, a quiet battle raged over where to bury the president. Lincoln's old

After Lincoln was buried in a simple vault on the side of a hill, some artists imagined a grander tomb for him. This was one idea, complete with a giant statue, that was never built.

hometown had won the prize: it would get to keep its most famous son. Local leaders wanted to build a large tomb in the center of Springfield, but Mary Lincoln had other ideas.

Years earlier, the Lincolns had joined their neighbors to open a new cemetery outside of town. Oak Ridge Cemetery was green, peaceful, and far away from the business and politics of downtown Springfield. This is where Mary wanted her husband to be laid to rest.

Despite the pleas of the city fathers that Lincoln deserved a splendid tomb where visitors could easily come and pay their respects, Mary had the final word. She gave Springfield a choice: bury Lincoln at Oak Ridge, or she would have his body taken to Chicago instead. Springfield surrendered; Lincoln would go to Oak Ridge.

But first his body was taken to the state capitol, right across from the law office he had shared with his partner, William H. Herndon. Above its windows hung a sign: "He Lives in the Hearts of His People." Nearby was his brother-in-law's store, where he had written his first inaugural address. And a few blocks to the east was the only house that he and Mary had ever owned. Now it was draped with black, and the neighbors were having their pictures taken out front. These were Lincoln's buildings, Lincoln's streets, Lincoln's people.

Lincoln had known this state capitol well. Here he had served as a state legislator, studied law books in the library, and kept an office after he was elected president. Inside the very chamber where his coffin was now placed, he had given one of his most famous speeches. Rising to accept the Republican nomination for the U.S. Senate in 1858, he had told his audience, "A house divided against itself cannot stand." He had been proved right. The divided house had fallen, but Lincoln had put it back together. And then he had paid with his life.

Thousands of his old friends and neighbors swarmed inside the capitol to look at his face for the last time. Lilacs filled the room. For years thereafter, local residents could not smell lilacs without thinking of Lincoln and that day.

On May 4, the coffin was taken to Oak Ridge and, with Willie's coffin, placed inside a vault on the side of a small hill in the center of the cemetery. Years later, a large marble monument would be built atop the hill to hold their bodies. For now, the burial was simple and quiet, just as Mary wished.

Lincoln was laid to rest in this burial vault at Oak Ridge Cemetery in Springfield, Illinois. The vault is still there, although the president's body was later moved.

With Robert Lincoln standing closest to the vault, the service began. Hymns were sung. Prayers were recited. Bishop Matthew Simpson of the Springfield Methodist Church gave the sermon. He wondered aloud why so many people had thronged to pay their respects to Lincoln in cities from Washington to Springfield. Bishop Simpson thought he knew the answer. "He made all men feel a sense of himself," he told them. And they, in turn, "saw in him a man who they believed would do what is right."

The mourners recited a final prayer, the tomb was locked, and Abraham Lincoln's long journey home was over.

Chapter Seven

Revenge and Justice

Somehow, with some two thousand soldiers searching for him, John Wilkes Booth managed to escape into the Confederacy. Dr. Samuel Mudd had sent him off as soon as he had learned that the soldiers were looking for him. But first Booth shaved off his mustache. Now he looked like a different man.

Rumors flew: Someone said that he had seen Booth in Washington, another in Pennsylvania, yet another in Chicago. Perhaps he was disguised as a woman or on his way to Canada.

Booth stayed out of sight. Then, after five days of hiding in the woods of southern Maryland, he and Davy Herold got hold of an old rowboat and crossed the river into Virginia on April 23. If Booth thought that he would be greeted like a hero when he landed in Virginia, he was sadly mistaken.

Trapped in Virginia

Booth could not understand why more people did not congratulate him for killing Lincoln. To one doctor in Virginia who did not want to help him, he wrote bitterly, "I would not have turned a dog from my door in such a condition." But Lee had surrendered, and the Union army now controlled the state. Even its most stubborn Confederates were unlikely to voice support for Lincoln's murderer. It was too dangerous.

"After being hunted like a dog through swamps, woods, and last night being chased by gun boats," Booth scribbled angrily in his diary, ". . . I am here in despair. And why; For doing what Brutus was honored for. . . . And yet I for striking down a greater tyrant . . . am looked upon as a common cutthroat."

"My action was purer . . . ," he ranted. "I do not repent the blow I struck. I may before God but not to man. I think I have done well, though I am abandoned, with the curse of Cain upon me."

"I have too great a soul to die like a criminal," he continued. "Let me die bravely."

On April 23, Booth and Herold broke into the home of a free black man named William Lucas. The desperate men forced Lucas out of the house so that they could hide there. The next day, they crossed the Rappahannock River by ferry. On the other shore, three former Confederate soldiers took Booth and Herold to the tobacco farm of a man named Richard H. Garrett on the main road near the town of Port Royal. When they arrived, Garrett and his son told the men that they could stay there.

Two days later, on April 26, a platoon of twenty-six Union cavalrymen tracked down the "abandoned" murderer to the remote little farm. At first Garrett would not tell the soldiers where Booth was hiding. But when the men tied a rope around his neck and swore that they would hang him then and there, Garrett's son quickly pointed to the barn.

Colonel E. J. Conger, the officer in charge, immediately ordered his men to surround the barn and shouted, "We know who you are! Surrender yourselves!" Herold gave up immediately, throwing down his gun and rushing outside with his hands in the air, whimpering. The soldiers quickly placed him under arrest and tied him to a nearby tree.

Booth refused to come out. He would never surrender, he shouted back. "You may prepare a stretcher for me," he yelled. "Draw up your men in a line, and let's have a fair fight." In his mind, he had done too much and come too far to be captured without one final, brave struggle.

So Colonel Conger set fire to the barn to force Booth out. Almost at once, flames shot up and engulfed the wooden building. Booth was trapped. The soldiers crept closer, and as the old walls burned and crumbled away, some could see Booth inside. One of the men, Sergeant Boston Corbett, thought he saw the assassin raise his pistol as if to shoot at the soldiers. In an instant, Corbett fired a shot into the barn. His bullet passed through Booth's neck, and Lincoln's murderer collapsed in a heap on the floor. The soldiers then braved the fire, racing inside to pull Booth from the barn just before it collapsed.

Dragged to Garrett's porch, unable to walk, Booth

Cornered in a burning Virginia barn, Booth was shot by Sergeant Boston Corbett. He died a few hours later.

Boston Corbett, who killed John Wilkes Booth, became a northern hero, but he later went insane.

gasped for water. He asked the colonel to kill him, but Conger refused. There was nothing to do but wait. The assassin lived for another three hours. When Booth was near death, he said, "Tell . . . my . . . Mother . . . I . . . die . . . for my country." Then he spoke his final words— "useless, useless"—and was dead.

While Lincoln's body was being carried in reverence through the North, his murderer's body was taken back to Washington in secret. There it was identified by doctors as Booth and buried in a sack under a jail cell beneath the Washington Penitentiary. When the jail was torn down two years later, Booth's remains were reburied at a nearby warehouse. Not until 1869 did the government return Booth's body to his family to be buried in the family plot in Baltimore, where it remains today. No tombstone marks the grave.

The Trial of the Century

The other members of Booth's gang were quickly rounded up, placed in chains, and charged with plotting the murder of President Lincoln.

Ned Spangler, the Ford's Theatre stagehand, was arrested on April 17. Later that day, Michael O'Laughlen and Samuel Arnold were captured, too. And that night, Lewis Powell and Mary Surratt were taken prisoner. George Atzerodt was tracked down at his cousin's house in Germantown, Maryland, on April 20. Dr. Mudd was taken into custody, too. He was the only accused man with a wife and family.

Learning of the assassination, John Surratt fled his hiding

place in upstate New York. He made his way to Canada and then to Europe, and was not heard from for two years.

Back in Washington, the prisoners were treated cruelly, but the public did not seem to care. Northerners were in a rage about the assassination and hungry for revenge. Secretary of War Stanton declared, "The stain of innocent blood must be removed from the land."

As spring turned into another blazing Washington summer, the prisoners were kept in tiny jail cells, closely guarded by four soldiers each. They were not allowed to speak to one another. To make sure they could not exchange messages, they were separated by empty prison cells. Their hands were kept in stiff metal handcuffs,

Secretary of State Seward's would-be murderer, Lewis Powell, was manacled after his capture. At the assassination trial, the handsome ex–Confederate soldier was the center of attention.

and their feet were attached to heavy iron balls and chains. For a time, many of them were forced to wear heavy canvas hoods that left them unable to speak and barely able to see.

The trial began on May 9, 1865, and lasted for almost two months. At first it was held in secret, but when the press objected, the courtroom was opened to reporters.

A nine-man military court served as both judge and jury. As the government explained, when Lincoln died, he was still commander in chief of the army and navy in time of war. The Booth gang was not entitled to a civilian trial.

As the trial dragged on in the stifling courtroom, some 340 witnesses testified about the complicated plot to murder Lincoln. Several blamed the former head of the Confederacy, Jefferson Davis, who by then was being held in another military prison off the coast of Virginia. The accused sat together, separated by guards, at a long table on a little stage at the front of the courtroom. They never said a word in their own defense.

To no one's surprise, they were all found guilty. Powell, Herold, Atzerodt, and Mary Surratt were sentenced to death by hanging. Mudd, Arnold, and O'Laughlen were sentenced to life in prison at one of the country's most horrible, disease-infested jails: Fort Jefferson, on a steamy, remote island off Key West, Florida. Spangler was sentenced to six years there.

No woman had ever been executed by the United States, and some Americans were shocked at the idea that Surratt would be put to death. President Johnson could have spared her life and sentenced her to life in prison instead, but he refused to change the sentence. As the new president said, Surratt had "kept the nest that hatched the rotten egg."

On July 7, 1865, Powell, Herold, Atzerodt, and

Surratt were hanged in the yard outside the jailhouse in Washington. Abraham Lincoln's murderers had paid for their crime with their lives.

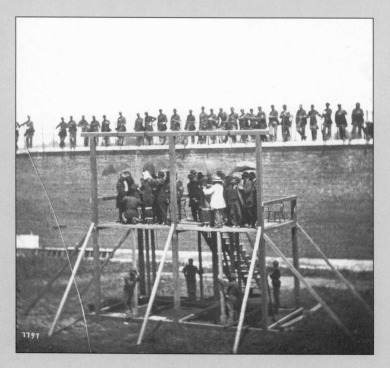

Execution of the Conspirators

Mary Surratt, Lewis Powell, David Herold, and George Atzerodt were hanged on July 7, 1865, in the yard of the old Washington prison. Photographer Alexander Gardner was allowed to take this picture of their execution. Until the very last minute, many Americans expected Surratt to be spared.

So Why Was Lincoln Murdered?

The truth is, much as Lincoln was loved by so many Americans, he was also deeply hated by others. More than half of the voters in the 1860 election voted against Lincoln. The South left the country as soon as he was elected. And, as president, he turned the country upside down: he drafted young men into the army, ended slavery, and for a time took away some constitutional rights.

Once the Union won the war, most southerners wanted simply to return to their homes, but others longed to strike back. Even some northerners understood this. As one Albany, New York, man said, "Abraham Lincoln was killed because he . . . trampled upon the laws of the country."

Still, once the war ended, Lincoln probably would not have lost his life had Booth remained onstage. Instead, hungry for glory, Booth became involved with Confederate agents and then planned a kidnapping plot that might have helped the southern cause by freeing Confederate prisoners from Union jails. Once the fighting stopped, however, Booth was on his own. He drank, he brooded, and he became obsessed with killing the president.

Why exactly did John Wilkes Booth decide to murder Abraham Lincoln? And how did he manage to succeed?

Booth killed because he was angry and frustrated. He already had popularity; now he wanted to be part of history. He refused to admit that the Civil War was over, refused to accept that the South had lost. He hated the idea that blacks might now become equal to whites. He wanted to turn back the clock, and he believed that most white people shared his feelings and would hail Lincoln's assassin as a hero. Instead, Booth helped turn Lincoln into one of the greatest heroes America has ever known. His killer, on the other hand, has gone down in history as the villain who robbed the country of its greatest president.

Booth believed that by killing Lincoln, he could keep the Confederacy alive. This is ironic, because the only reason he succeeded is because the Confederacy was dead. After Lee surrendered, Lincoln's friends and advisers let down their guard. Few people, least of all Lincoln, believed that his life was in danger, and security became lax.

Was Booth part of a grand scheme by Confederate leaders to start the war all over again? Not by the time he shot Lincoln. Earlier, perhaps, the Confederate government had encouraged Booth, but not after Lee's surrender. By then, Lincoln wanted to heal the country, and most southerners wanted the bloodshed to come to an end.

Had Booth never struck—had someone stopped him—had he lost his nerve—if Lincoln had lived—what would our history be?

Would black Americans have gained more freedoms more quickly? Would the struggles of the civil rights movement one hundred years later have been unnecessary? Would Reconstruction have been less painful for both North and South? We will never know the answers to these questions.

Lincoln's murder taught America many lessons. Perhaps the most important is that any effort to bring about monumental change may carry with it a great price. Lincoln changed our country, but he died as a result of his efforts.

Postscript

What Became of . . . ?

Mary Todd Lincoln never recovered from the shock of her husband's murder. She remained in what she called "intense misery." The president's widow stayed locked inside the White House for five weeks, then moved to Chicago, where she fought often with her son Robert and his new wife. In 1875, Robert had his mother tried for insanity. She was judged insane and placed in a mental institution for nearly a year. The court later set her free. She then wandered through Europe alone and finally moved back to Springfield. She lived out her final days with her sister in the house where she had married Lincoln forty years before, dying in 1882. From the day Booth murdered her husband at Ford's to the day she died seventeen years later, Mary Lincoln never set foot in a theater again.

Tad Lincoln, "full of merry mischief," suffered from learning disabilities and speech problems. After his father's death, his health declined. He died in 1871 at the age of eighteen, sending his mother into another desperate period of grief.

Robert Lincoln went on to become a lawyer, a cabinet secretary under two presidents, and an ambassador to England. He was a successful businessman, earning millions in railroads. But he had a troubled personal life. Worried about his mother's safety—and perhaps her money, as well—he had Mary put on trial, declared insane, and committed to a mental hospital. Even though she left less than a year later, they never were close again. Robert's only son, Abraham Lincoln II, died when he was a teenager. Robert is the only member of President Lincoln's family of four sons who is not buried in the Lincoln tomb in Springfield. He is buried at Arlington National Cemetery in Virginia.

Andrew Johnson proved a dismal failure as president. Lincoln's old supporters felt that Johnson wanted to rob African Americans of the few civil rights they enjoyed. When Johnson tried to fire Secretary of War Edwin Stanton without first winning the approval of Congress, he was impeached. The Senate failed to convict Johnson and remove him from office, but his presidency was destroyed. Mary Lincoln forever suspected him of being part of the plot to kill her husband. Johnson returned to Washington in 1875 as a senator from his home state of Tennessee. He died later that year.

General Ulysses S. Grant became the eighteenth president of the United States in 1869. He served two terms, overseeing the Reconstruction of the South. He later lost all his money in a bad business deal. Stricken with throat cancer, he raced to finish his memoirs before he died in 1885. The book became a bestseller and earned his family a fortune.

Edwin M. Stanton, who took charge of the country after Booth shot Lincoln, wanted desperately to end his career on the U.S. Supreme Court. President Grant finally fulfilled this dream in 1869, but just a few days after he was confirmed as an associate justice, Stanton died. In 1937, a book about the Lincoln assassination blamed Stanton for the crime and accused him of being part of Booth's plot. Though untrue and unfair, some people still believe the theory today.

William H. Seward watched Lincoln's funeral procession in Washington from his sickbed. He eventually recovered from both his carriage accident and the attack by Lewis Powell. Seward returned to his post as secretary of state under President Johnson. His greatest accomplishment was America's purchase of Alaska from Russia in 1867. Seward died in Auburn, New York, in 1872.

Jefferson Davis, America's "other" Civil War president, fled from Richmond in April 1865. He was captured the following month in Irwinville, Georgia. He served two years in prison at Fort Monroe, Virginia. After his release, he continued to speak out about the "Lost Cause" of the Confederacy until his death in 1889. Although Stanton wanted Americans to believe that Davis was behind the plot to murder Lincoln, no one has ever found a shred of proof that Davis was personally or directly involved with Booth and his gang.

Robert E. Lee, whose photograph Lincoln studied the day he was shot, became president of Washington College in Lexington, Virginia. He died there in 1870.

Michael O'Laughlen, Booth's childhood friend, died of yellow fever at Fort Jefferson prison in 1867.

Samuel Arnold, sentenced to life in prison for plotting with Booth, was pardoned by President Andrew Johnson in 1869. In 1902, the aging Arnold wrote a story about the Lincoln kidnapping plot for a Baltimore newspaper. The article insisted that the original plan to carry Lincoln to Richmond had been "patriotic." Few people paid attention. Arnold died four years later at the age of seventy-two.

Dr. Samuel Mudd was pardoned by President Johnson in 1869 for his "care and cure of the sick" when yellow fever struck Fort Jefferson prison. Back home in Maryland, Mudd spent the rest of his life maintaining his innocence. He died in 1883 at the age of forty-nine. One of his thirty-two grandchildren, Richard Mudd, later led the family's long crusade to clear Mudd's name, until his own death at the age of 101 in 2002.

Ned Spangler also was pardoned in 1869. The Mudd family took him in, and for the rest of his days, he worked as a handyman on their farm. He died there in 1875.

John H. Surratt fled to Europe and joined the Papal Guards in Rome. Tipped off that he had been located, he fled to Egypt, where he was arrested in 1866. Taken back to the United States to face charges, Surratt was never convicted of a crime. Later he worked as a clerk at a Baltimore steamship company. He was the last surviving member of Booth's gang when he died in 1916.

Major Henry Rathbone and **Clara Harris**, the Lincolns' guests at Ford's Theatre the night of the assassination, were married in 1867. Rathbone was deeply troubled by the events he had witnessed, and he never forgave himself for failing to save Lincoln's life. He suffered from several mental breakdowns, and in 1883, while living in Germany, he lost his mind completely, attacked his three children, stabbed Clara to death, and tried to kill himself. He told doctors he had seen people "hiding behind the pictures on the wall." Rathbone spent the rest of his life in an insane asylum in Germany. He died there in 1911 at the age of seventy-three. The tragic life of the Rathbones recently inspired a novel and an opera.

Sergeant Boston Corbett and the Union soldiers at Garrett's farm in Virginia had been ordered not to shoot Booth, but Corbett later said that God had told him to fire the shot that killed Lincoln's assassin. He became a hero in the North but eventually lost his mind. Later, serving as an honorary guard at a mock session of the Kansas state legislature, he began shooting at the interns, pages, and clerks. He was confined to the Topeka Asylum for the Insane but escaped in 1888. No one knows what became of him.

Ford's Theatre was closed down on the orders of Secretary of War Stanton right after Lincoln's assassination, and **John T. Ford** was thrown into jail for thirty-nine days. Once free, Ford tried to reopen his theater in July, just after the conspirators were hanged. The public reacted so angrily that he canceled his plans. Ford blamed the government for ruining him and demanded that it pay him for lost business. The War Department agreed to rent, then buy, his building and turned it into office space. Tragedy struck there again in June 1893, when the upper floors suddenly collapsed into the basement, killing twenty-two workers and injuring sixty-eight. The interior was rebuilt yet again, and Ford's became a Lincoln museum in the 1920s. Forty years later, the building was restored to the way it looked the night Lincoln was murdered. In 1968, Ford's reopened as a theater for the first time in 103 years. Performances have been taking place there ever since. Today the presidential box looks just as it did on April 14, 1865, complete with flags and furniture. Out of respect for Lincoln's memory, no one is allowed to sit there. Items related to the assassination, including the gun that Booth used to kill Lincoln, are on display in a museum in the theater's basement.

The Petersen house, where Lincoln died, remained in the Petersen family until the 1870s. It was later bought by a newspaper editor and then sold to Washington's Memorial Association in the late 1800s. Today it is open to the public. Visitors can see the tiny room where the president died and the parlor where Mary Lincoln waited through the night and prayed that her husband would recover.

Abraham Lincoln as he looked about 15 months before his murder—in a photo taken in Washington on January 8, 1864.

Abraham Lincoln was the first American president to be assassinated but not the last. James A. Garfield was killed in 1881, William McKinley in 1901, and John F. Kennedy in 1963. Theodore Roosevelt was shot at in 1912 but was not hurt. An assassin barely missed killing Franklin D. Roosevelt before he became president in 1933. Two murder attempts were made on President Gerald Ford, and President Ronald Reagan was shot in 1981. Today Secret Service protection of the president is very tight, and access to him is carefully controlled. Abraham Lincoln saved the Union, but his murder changed the presidency—and the country—forever.

Bibliography

(* = illustrated book)

Alford, Terry, ed. *John Wilkes Booth: A Sister's Memoirs*. Jackson: University Press of Mississippi, 1996.

Bak, Richard, ed. *The Day Lincoln Was Shot: An Illustrated Chronicle*. Dallas: Taylor Publishing, 1998.*

Browne, Francis F. *The Everyday Life of Abraham Lincoln*. Hartford: Park Publishing Co., 1886.

Chesebrough, David B. *"No Sorrow Like Our Sorrow": Northern Protestant Ministers and the Assassination of Abraham Lincoln*. Kent, Ohio: Kent State University Press, 1994.

Cuomo, Mario M., and Harold Holzer. *Lincoln on Democracy*. New York: HarperCollins, 1990.

Ford's Theatre and the Lincoln Assassination. Alexandria, Va.: Parks & History Association, 2001.*

Furtwangler, Albert. *Assassin on Stage*. Urbana: University of Illinois Press, 1991.

Good, Timothy S. *We Saw Lincoln Shot: One Hundred Eyewitness Accounts*. Jackson: University Press of Mississippi, 1995.

Gutman, Richard J. S., and Kellie O. Gutman. *John Wilkes Booth Himself*. Dover, Mass.: Hired Hand Press, 1979.*

Hanchett, William. *The Lincoln Murder Conspiracies*. Urbana: University of Illinois Press, 1983.

Harrell, Carolyn. *When the Bells Tolled for Lincoln: Southern Reaction to the Assassination*. Macon, Ga.: Mercer University Press, 1997.

Holzer, Harold. *Dear Mr. Lincoln: Letters to the President*. New York: Addison Wesley, 1993.

———. *The Lincoln Mailbag*. Carbondale: Southern Illinois University Press, 1998.

Holzer, Harold, Mark E. Neely, and Gabor S. Boritt. *The Lincoln Image: Abraham Lincoln and the Popular Print*. New York: Scribner's, 1984.*

Holzer, Harold, and Frank J. Williams. *Lincoln's Deathbed in Art and Memory: The "Rubber Room" Phenomenon*. Gettysburg, Pa.: Thomas Publications, 1998.*

Jakoubek, Robert E. *The Assassination of Abraham Lincoln*. Brookfield, Conn.: Millbrook Press, 1993.

Kunhardt, Dorothy Meserve, and Philip B. Kunhardt. *Twenty Days*. New York: Harper & Row, 1965.*

Lewis, Lloyd. *The Assassination of Lincoln: History and Myth*. 1929. Reprint, Lincoln: University of Nebraska Press, 1994.

Lorant, Stefan. *Lincoln: A Picture Story of His Life*. Rev. ed. New York: W. W. Norton, 1969.

O'Neal, Michael. *The Assassination of Abraham Lincoln*. San Diego: Greenhaven Press, 1991.

Ownsbey, Betty. *Alias "Paine": Lewis Thornton Powell, the Mystery Man of the Lincoln Conspiracy*. Jefferson, N.C.: McFarland, 1993.

Reck, W. Emerson. *A. Lincoln: His Last 24 Hours*. Jefferson, N.C.: McFarland, 1987.

Rhodehamel, John, and Louise Taper, eds. *"Right or Wrong, God Judge Me": The Writings of John Wilkes Booth*. Urbana: University of Illinois Press, 1997.

Steers, Edward Jr. *Blood on the Moon: The Assassination of Abraham Lincoln*. Lexington: University Press of Kentucky, 2001.

———. *His Name Is Still Mudd*. Gettysburg, Pa.: Thomas Publications, 1997.

Swanson, James L., and Daniel R. Weinberg. *Lincoln's Assassins: Their Trial and Execution*. Santa Fe, N.M.: Arena Editions, 2001.*

Tidwell, William A. *April '65: Confederate Covert Action in the American Civil War*. Kent, Ohio: Kent State University Press, 1995.

Tidwell, William A., with James O. Hall and David Winfred Gaddy. *Come Retribution: The Confederate Secret Service and the Assassination of Lincoln*. Jackson: University Press of Mississippi, 1988.

Turner, Thomas Reed. *Beware the People Weeping: Public Opinion and the Assassination of Abraham Lincoln*. Baton Rouge: Louisiana State University Press, 1982.

Weichmann, Louis J. *A True History of the Assassination of Abraham Lincoln and of the Conspiracy of 1865*. Edited by Floyd Risvold. New York: Alfred A. Knopf, 1975.

Zeinert, Karen. *The Lincoln Murder Plot*. North Haven, Conn.: Linnet Books, 1999.

General References

Basler, Roy P., ed. *The Collected Works of Abraham Lincoln*. 8 vols. New Brunswick, N.J.: Rutgers University Press, 1953–1955.

Donald, David Herbert. *Lincoln*. New York: Simon & Schuster, 1995.

Fehrenbacher, Don E., and Virginia Fehrenbacher. *Recollected Words of Abraham Lincoln*. Stanford, Calif.: Stanford University Press, 1996.

Miers, Earl Schenck, ed. *Lincoln Day by Day: A Chronology, 1809–1865*. 3 vols. Washington, D.C.: Lincoln Sesquicentennial Commission, 1959. Reprint, Dayton, Oh.: Morningside Books, 1991.

Turner, Justin, and Linda Levitt Turner. *Mary Todd Lincoln: Her Life and Letters*. New York: Alfred A. Knopf, 1972.

Welles, Gideon. *Diary*. 3 vols. Boston: Houghton Mifflin, 1911.

Places to Visit

On the day of his hometown funeral, Lincoln's old house in Springfield, Illinois, was draped in black. This was the only home Lincoln ever owned.

Clinton, Maryland
Surratt House Museum

Fort Wayne, Indiana
The Lincoln Museum

New York, New York
City Hall
Edwin Booth's home (The Player's Club)

Redlands, California
The Lincoln Memorial Shrine

Springfield, Illinois
Abraham Lincoln Presidential Library and Museum
*   (scheduled to open in 2005)*
The Lincoln-Herndon Law Offices
The Lincoln Home National Historic Site
The Lincoln Tomb, Oak Ridge Cemetery
The Old State Capitol

Waldorf, Maryland
Dr. Samuel A. Mudd House

Washington, D.C.
Ford's Theatre National Historic Site and
*   Museum of the Assassination*
Petersen House
The White House

Index